A Day in the Life of Ancient Rome

by

Hilary J. Deighton

Bristol Classical Press

First published in 1992
Revised edition published in 1996 by
Bristol Classical Press
an imprint of
Gerald Duckworth & Co. Ltd.
The Old Piano Factory
48 Hoxton Square, London N1 6PB

A catalogue record of this book is available
from the British Library

ISBN 1-85399-136-8

Available in USA and Canada from:
Focus Information Group
PO Box 369
Newburyport
MA 01950

Printed in Great Britain by
Booksprint, Bristol

For Alan and Jeremy

Contents

Preface

This is a book about the other great questions of history – not about the elegance of Horace's poetry, but the sort of thing he would have for dinner; not about Augustus' frontier policy, but the sort of latrines he would use. It is a response to the burning curiosity of the adventurer into the past: what was it like actually to *be* there? I hope that by the end of this book the reader may feel that he/she has spent the day in ancient Rome, walked in the streets and met the people.

Within the confines of a short volume one has to be painfully selective. This book is specifically about the life of the people of Rome itself, and at a certain period – the late Republic and early Empire (although evidence is out of necessity adduced from farther afield). It is also specifically about the fascinating but often neglected details of daily living – a student may complete a degree in Classics with hardly an idea about Roman food or furniture, and this is an attempt to bridge this gap for the specialist Classicist, the student of Classical Civilisation, and the increasing number of people who come to the study of the Classical world later in life, in the Open University or evening classes – or just for fun. It cannot, in so brief a space, be a complete account, but I hope it may fire the imagination.

My thanks are due to many people – most of all perhaps to my own Open University students, whose interest, enthusiasm and questions were the inspiration for the book. I must also thank the editors at Bristol Classical Press for their patience and support. I am grateful to Georgina Plowright of Newcastle University and C.J. Fance, Head of Classics at Bristol Cathedral School, for their helpful comments. Any remaining imperfections are entirely my responsibility. Last, but far from least, I owe a special debt of gratitude to Linda Hennessy for her delightful recreations of Roman life in the illustrations.

Bristol
January 1991

A Day in the Life . . .

The first hour, and the second, exhaust clients on their morning
    visits,
The third keeps the shyster lawyers busy,
Up to the fifth Rome passes the time in various labours,
The sixth brings languid quietness, everything stops at the
    seventh,
The eighth and ninth are wrestling-time for those in good
    condition,
The ninth bids us sink into the cushions piled on the dinner
    couches:
The tenth is the hour for my scribblings, Euphemus,
And you have the charge of mixing the ambrosia for the feast,
While noble Caesar relaxes with a moderate cupful in his great
    hand.
Then bring on my jokes: will you let Jove get them by morning,
    Thalia, our Comic Muse?

Martial IV.8

List of Illustrations

Introduction

Early morning in Rome was a pretty noisy event, so the poet Martial tells us, and this should not come as a surprise. Martial may have spent part of his morning recovering from the hospitality of a generous patron the night before, which could have soured his outlook, but it is not hard to see his point.

Then, as now, life in Mediterranean countries is determined as much by climate as culture, and the two are necessarily interwoven. People are up with the dawn for the very good reason that the heat of mid-day in summer makes working barely tolerable, and not particularly sensible. The Romans liked to get their business attended to in the morning.

Wheeled traffic was forbidden in the city during daylight hours – there was not the space in the narrow, crowded streets – but there would be pack animals bringing goods to market, and clattering over the paving stones. The bakers would be up and busy, as would the proprietors of the many Roman equivalents of fast food stalls – bars, hot food shops, the ancient equivalents of the modern Roman pizza shop on every street corner. The barbers would be setting up business on the streets, for the convenience of those without suitable slaves to perform this service. Tradesmen and craftsmen would be setting out their wares or setting up their workshops.

Add to all this clamour the sounds of neighbours rising, talking, quarrelling, buying breakfast from the prepared-food shops, and we can start to sympathise with Martial. The majority of the Roman people did not live in villas – cool, inward-looking oases in a huge, crowded, bustling city – but in apartment blocks, or *insulae* (Fig. 1, see p. 10). The apartments could vary considerably in size and comfort, but as anyone who has ever lived in a flat well knows, sound travels.

Many modern European cities have lost this sense of crowding together, shared bustle and noise, but around the Mediterranean,

Figure 1. An *insula* with a garden court.

in the cities of Southern Europe, Africa and Asia one can still sense what such a place must have been like.

How would a family have faced its day? The people for whom we have the most information, of course, are the better-off – the literate, if not literary, the notable and the noticeable, the powerful, the litigious. It is a simple fact of history, though not of archaeology, that these are the people who are able to leave us the story of their times, in poetry and prose, imperial edicts and law cases, historical and scientific studies, in letters. They employed the leather-workers, painters, sculptors, jewellers and masons, but do not, on the whole, go into much detail about the people who produced that which adorned or facilitated their lives. For the rest we must depend on the graffiti, the shop signs, the advertising posters (yes, Rome too had all of these) and such incidental small treasures.

When we consider the archaeological, as well as the purely historical evidence, the picture does balance out. The dwellings and workshops of the humble remain alongside the grandiose homes and follies of the wealthy. It is a rather uncomfortable fact of archaeology that there is nothing so beneficial to the modern scholar as a thorough-going disaster. When a site is abandoned naturally, people take their gods and their cooking pots and their furniture with them. When a place falls, by invasion or natural disaster, then not only are the gods, the cooking pots and the furniture (if not looted) left scattered, but also some of the people as well. For the study of Roman life we are fortunate in the misfortunes of the wretched people of Pompeii and Herculaneum, the one covered with ash and pumice, the other in solidified burning mud. For those who did not take the chance to leave at the first warning, the end came so swiftly that we are left with an extraordinary snapshot of a day in ordinary lives – half-eaten meals, sick children abed, newly-baked bread awaiting the customer.

In this book we shall be looking at ordinary, everyday life – not at 'social life' and social issues, but daily life – what it was like to be a Roman.

There are, however, one or two general points that have to be made at the outset about social conditions. One thing is the ubiquity and vital importance of slaves. The economy was founded on slavery. In terms of technological skill and intellect the Romans were quite capable of having an industrial revolution, but there was never any perceived necessity. Labour was free, at least in terms of salary costs, and it was everywhere. Slaves did, of course, have to be bought or bred, clothed, housed, fed and watered. Seneca grumbled about the cost of maintaining his slaves. Cato treats the running costs and disposal of slaves in the same terms as cattle or agricultural machinery. The number of slaves (and freedmen) in Rome was so great that a proposal to have them uniformly dressed was rejected for precisely the reason that such visibility would make them realise their strength in numbers. The presence of slaves in every sphere and at every level – from positions of enormous influence in the Imperial household to utter misery on the great ranches or *latifundia* – had a profound effect on Roman society.

A second feature of Roman life, which need not be dwelt on here, but which will be seen to manifest itself in practical and visible daily detail, is the strict division of Roman society into classes, defined by political office and by their financial ranking. At the top was the senatorial class, followed by the *equites* (the knights), and then the people. The old division between patrician and plebeian had really ceased to have any force by Imperial times. The old patrician ranks had pretty well been wiped out over the course of the series of vicious civil wars that convulsed the late Republic.

A third aspect of Roman life is something for which it is hard to find a modern parallel – the truly staggering wealth in the hands of the powerful. Julius Caesar, as one example, was able to leave a significant sum of money to each and every Roman citizen in his will; Marcus Agrippa undertook huge public building programmes at his own expense. In the time of Cato the Censor, a labourer could expect to get by on about 300 denarii a year, while at the same time Scipio Africanus was reckoned to be worth a million. Crassus the *triumvir*, Caesar's contemporary and occasional colleague, had real estate to a value of 50 million denarii. Some parallels might be seen in plutocratic America perhaps, or the princely states of India, or the oil sheikhs. The economy of Rome was bolstered by empire and conquest rather than by production and domestic agriculture – not a wholly safe basis for an economy it must be said, but it is worth remembering that there was vast wealth in Rome. Not everyone had a share of it (the pacification of a large population of potentially-destabilising disaffected urban poor regularly had occasion to concentrate the minds of Rome's masters by the late Republic, and especially in the Imperial period). But for those who were wealthy the living was easy, and it was, like slavery, a factor contributing to the corruption, *ennui* and excess for which life at the top in Rome is famed (not *always* justly), as well as to a graciousness and elegance of living that holds its appeal to this day. Indeed, if one could find an intact Roman villa going spare, complete with central heating, running water, sanitary arrangements better than modern ones in many parts of the world, and not least Europe, it is likely one would need only the addition of electricity, perhaps the comforts of modern plumbing and replacement of lead pipes, to make it a very desirable home for anyone today with a taste for privacy, comfort and gardening.

The fourth and last 'given' of social, as opposed to daily life which should underscore the details in this book is the patron–client relationship. This is again something that permeates the whole of society, and with its code of mutual ties and responsibilities smacks of an earlier tribal culture, rather than the urbanised, developed society of Rome. Because so much in Rome appears easily accessible and understandable, elements of its alienness come as a shock. This is one such. It was a serious and important relationship, and a cohesive force in society (indeed in Imperial times the Emperor could be seen as having the whole *populus* as his clients). The system was, of course, open to abuse on both sides. The relationship did, however, have its place in everyday life, as we shall see.

So how would a family have faced its day? For reasons which should now be obvious, we shall be more concerned with the life of a moderately well-off family – these are the people we know most about – but the broader spectrum should still be visible.

Morning

The Romans would rise early: father to set about his business affairs, sons and pre-pubescent daughters to be educated. In a moderately well-off household the mistress of the house would probably not require or wish to be up at or before dawn. Any domestic tasks to be attended to would be the duties of slaves.

The immediate process of getting up and dressed would not be a complex one, however. A man or child would have slept in his tunic and, depending on status, intentions for the day and time of year, would not have much more to don. A slave or labourer would wear a short tunic, perhaps with a heavier over-tunic in winter, reaching down almost to his ankles. This could be plain, or richly decorated, in wool of differing weights, or even silk from India, or indeed China (rather bad form for men, but that would not deter the indulgent). Cotton was rare, despite contact with Egypt where fine cotton was produced in the same places and by the same methods then as now – although the old ways are disappearing. The Greek island of Kos was an entrepôt for the silk trade, and a textile combining silk and linen was manufactured there which was traded to Rome. Such fabrics were used more by women, but there are recorded instances of men dressed flamboyantly in rich colours and delicate fabrics. The fact that this was effete and unRoman may have been of some comfort to those who could not dream of affording them. In plainer versions the tunic could also be a demonstration of a man's place in society, as we shall see in the next chapter.

The tunic then, long and short, was the basic male Roman garment, easy and comfortable to wear (Fig. 2, see p. 15). These are two adjectives which could not be applied to the distinctive, and distinguishing, robe of the Roman citizen – the toga (Fig. 2). This cumbersome piece of clothing was synonymous with Rome and with civilisation; to wear the toga was to be civilised. You really did have to be one of the master race to wear it, because taking

Figure 2. The toga, the tunic, sandals and one-piece shoes.

part in any unseemly activity whilst so clad was unlikely to be possible. It was a large semi-circular length of cloth, made of wool, and therefore heavy, which was draped first over the left shoulder, wrapped round under the right arm, then back over the left shoulder – a little like a sari, but not so light, long or secure. Folds might be drawn over the head in protection, or as a gesture of reverence, as we see, for example, with the Imperial family depicted in religious solemnities on the *Ara Pacis*, Augustus' altar to Peace. A fold in the toga would also be used as a pocket. The toga was a visible statement of the wearer's rank.

The toga certainly looks very noble, and had a high symbolic value, but it was not a very practical garment. It fell progressively out of favour from the first century AD onwards. Tunics and cloaks became the more usual everyday dress.

Before donning his toga, a man might have a quick wash in cold water, not much more than a splash, as the real cleansing of the day would take place at the baths in the afternoon. He might clean his teeth with powdered pumice stone or powdered horn – this is not so different from tooth powder or smoker's toothpaste today, which contain abrasives that effectively render them flavoured scouring powder. For those for whom such expedients were no longer of any use, false teeth of ivory were available, set in gold bands.

The child getting up would be careful to put an amulet or bulla back on, if he or she had taken it off in the night. The wearing of tutelary images was common. They came in a variety of devices, but frequently in phallic form. The phallus being an important protective symbol in Rome as in Greece, it appeared as an apotropaic (i.e., turning away evil) symbol in many contexts, both personal and public. Amulets are found in pendant form, or sometimes as tiny rings, which may have been worn by very small children, or hung around the neck, placed there during the naming ceremony eight (for a girl) or nine (for a boy) days after birth. A free child would always be protected in this way. The bulla might be contained in a leather bag for the poor, or gold bag, for one of higher birth.

The lady of the house would have a more complicated set of undergarments. Female acrobats are depicted in bikini-like garments, although the top section is no more advanced in its concession to female form than a simple bandeau – the same shape is seen in wall-paintings (of a more privately athletic nature), mosaics, and mentioned in poetry. There are hints of greater corsetry skills available to women – Ovid (*Ars Amatoria*, III.274 -5) recommends padded underpinnings for the small-breasted. A very well-made leather bikini bottom has been found in London. This would almost certainly have been an entertainer's garment, but demonstrates the ability to make good underclothes. (The suggestion has been made that it might have been used as sanitary protection, but as we have pictorial evidence of a girl acrobat wearing something just like this, that seems to be a more likely explanation.) Roman women's clothes tended to the voluminous, so there was not a pressing need for detailed ability in corsetry. Breastbands, shifts and loincloths would be the most common undergarments. An over-tunic would be worn over the shift, and a dress over that. Before considering women's dress in detail, however, especially as the lady's levée and toilette would take longer than her husband's, let us pause a while and look around the bedroom (Fig. 3).

Figure 3.   A Roman bedroom.

In the smaller, cramped apartments of an *insula* (generally the higher the floor the smaller and cheaper the apartment) the luxury of separate bedrooms would not exist. In a villa, or a large apartment, say, a shopkeeper's home above his business premises, there would be separate bedrooms – not just for various members of the family, but for man and wife. Both archaeological and textual evidence suggests that a couple would not habitually sleep together. Beds are usually single, and rarely found two to a room, though evidence of two single beds in a room – at right angles and not together – has been found at Herculaneum. There does, on the other hand, exist a charming figurine from southern Gaul of a couple embracing in a bed that comfortably accommodates them both, with their pet dog lying at their feet. There are plenty of illustrations available of couples (coupling), but the evidence does seem to be that they came together only for the occasion, and normally slept in their separate rooms.

Beds were wooden, of a divan type, with mattresses placed on wooden slats, or sometimes rope webbing. They might have a surround on three sides (Figs 3 and 4, see pp. 17, 19), like the inlaid bed in the Shop of the Gem-Cutter, Herculaneum, which sadly contains the bones of its last occupant: a child, evidently unwell, and left in the care of a nurse, whose loom was set up at the bed-side. As the bones of the nurse were not found in the room, it would seem her devotion was not total. The decoration of surround and bed itself varied with economic standing – the legs might be well-turned and ornamented with filigree metal, or with wood inlay. A low wooden baby's cradle on rockers has also been preserved at Herculaneum – also containing its pathetic little bundle of bones. It has open, barred sides. Mattresses and pillows would be stuffed with wool, or perhaps straw or other vegetable packing, like sedge grass, and vary in depth and comfort according either to the taste or the finances of its owner. Evidence, for example, from scenes on grave stelae, suggests that many Romans and provincials saw no point in roughing it – deep, plump mattresses and pillows, carved bases, legs and surrounds and decorative textiles are all to be seen.

The bedroom itself would not be spacious. These were rooms used for the function of sleep, rather than boudoirs where friends might be received. A curious factor to modern perceptions is that

Figure 4.   A sarcophagus from Simpelveld decorated with a house scene.

these rooms (with paint remaining to show us), could be decorated in very dark colours, such as the deep Pompeian red, or even black (large washes of dark colour are particularly characteristic of what is known as the 'Third Style' of wall-painting [roughly the first two-thirds of the first century AD]). Although techniques of expanding a room space by *trompe l'oeil* design were well-understood, the Romans did not seem to have a taste, as many people nowadays would, for altering the perception of a room's space by the use of light colours. This may be a function of the fact that these rooms were not used for reception (although reception rooms too are profusely decorated), or partly because the construction of a Roman house round a garden or light well of some form, where possible, satisfied the need for light under a brilliant Mediterranean sky, or then just a matter of different taste. Given that Roman houses, as indeed Italian houses still are, would be designed more to take account of oppressive summer heat than rain-washed winters, the choice of dark colours which would reinforce and retain heat remains curious to us, even though the brighter light would, to an extent, absorb colour.

The truly wealthy and privileged could indulge in a choice of bedrooms – perhaps not in crowded Rome, but in a country or seaside retreat where more extravagant whims could be indulged, and there was space for expansion. Pliny the Younger, who, like others of his standing, had more than one place in the country, has left us letters in which he describes his out-of-town retreats in considerable detail. Amongst the enviable facilities are different bedrooms as well as dining-rooms to suit the seasons, and places to which he might withdraw during the day to escape the noise of the household.

Other room furnishings apart from the bed would be simple enough – chests for clothing and valuables, table, chair or stool, candelabrum. The mistress of the house might keep her small lockable box of valuables at her side as she sat to be coiffed and made up by her slaves, for the the first time that day. Repairs, or a complete remake, might be necessary after the afternoon bath, or after prolonged exposure to the weather. Ovid has left us some scathing comments on over-made-up women streaking their maquillage with sweat. Apart from presenting a fairly unappetising picture to the men their make-up should impress, these women were also risking injury from some of the substances they used for make-up, white lead being one of the most noxious.

Before her make-up could go on in the morning, however, the face-conscious lady would have to remove the bread and water face-pack she had applied the night before. This would help to preserve her complexion for her day-time lover, rather than the legal evening attentions of her husband, so this practice also comes in for some jaundiced comment. It must, of course, be remembered that while sources such as the erotic poets may contain many a gem of information, the purpose and nature of their work is bound to contain certain slants and biasses – many a perfectly respectable Roman woman may have taken care over her appearance without any intention of seeing with whom she could flirt at the races, or pick up on a visit to the temple (a prime place for assignations).

Combs, mirrors, perfume flasks, tweezers, little pots, spatulas and little mortars and pestles for make-up have all come down to us, as well as written evidence for the means women used to beautify themselves (Fig. 5, see p. 21). Paintings and especially portrait busts can also tell us a good deal about hairstyles. These, indeed, become so subject to changing fashion whims that they can

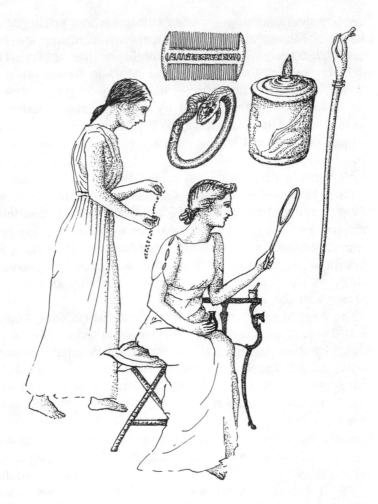

Figure 5.   A lady at her toilette with (inset) a comb, braclet, cosmetics pot and hairpin.

be used as dating techniques for the Imperial period, becoming (during the first and second centuries AD) so elaborate that they must have required considerable skill, patience and time to create, and a measure of determined strength to wear. That the skills did not always come up to expectation can be guessed from the fact that one finds more than one reference to an angry mistress jabbing a hairpin into the arm of her unfortunate slave, or hitting her with a mirror.

As for the Romans, as for other cultures with a privileged few, excess of leisure and often conspicuous consumption (e.g., eighteenth-century Europe), wigs might be the answer. These might be necessary not only to save hours in having one's hair dressed in an elaborate nature – and gravity-defying curls – but also to hide the damage caused by inimical beauty products, or careless use of the curling-tongs. The blonde hair of German captives was favoured for this purpose, as was black hair imported from India.

We shall, however, leave the lady of leisure and indulgence for a while, to see what the other members of the household were doing – remembering that not all women were leisured or indulged. For many Roman women, free or slaves, the day would begin with a quick wash, dressing, tying back one's hair and getting on with work, in or out of the home, and even the grandest of women would still have the ultimate responsibility for the smooth operation of the household.

The younger members of the household, the children, would be up at dawn, or even earlier in winter-time, in order to be taken to school by their *paidagogus*. This word, taken directly from the Greek, is often translated as 'tutor'. He would be a trusted slave, and might well be Greek, as the Romans were indebted to the Greeks for their education (their art, almost all of their literary forms and their medicine). It was his job to take a child to school, stay with him there, and bring him home. The role would probably extend to additional tuition, including that of the daughters. Girls of the higher ranks at least were certainly educated, and could go to school, but this was not as common as it was for boys. Having such a role, the *paidagogus* would obviously hold a special place in the household, and be amongst those for whom slavery was more a live-in job than wretched oppression.

He and his charge, or charges, would set off to the premises of the *litterator*, the teacher. What might be described as primary education took place from the age of about six or seven to early adolescence, and largely comprised the traditional three 'R's – reading, writing and 'rithmetic (which requires a lot more active thought in Roman numerals). Reading and writing would be in Greek as well as Latin, from the ages of about eleven to sixteen, when the child would study with a *grammaticus*, with Homer forming as much of a basis for education for the Roman as the Greek child. The study of the Homeric epics took some of the same places that might be filled in the modern curriculum by Bible Study, Shakespeare and the legends of King Arthur and the Holy Grail, and the well-educated man would be expected to be able to quote extensively. Under the Empire, Vergil would usurp some of this pre-eminence, but Greek literature remained the major source and pattern.

With a *paidagogus* at his side, the schoolboy would be unable to drag his feet, however apprehensive he might feel, but he would probably still find lots of diverting things to see on the way to take his mind off any possible impending confrontation with the school-master.

In the house there would be the usual early morning bustle, especially in the kitchens, for while breakfast was not much of a feature of the Roman day, many dishes required long and/or elaborate preparation and cooking. The major kind of activity, however, would be of a type unparalleled in modern western culture, and would take place in the master's study, the *tablinum* – the morning visit of the clients. The curious child might watch the procession of visitors, before being taken out into the streets, where in the summer there might still be some lingering coolness from the night. In the winter there would be warm woollen cloaks worn over the tunics, and broad-brimmed hats (country clothing really, but serviceable) to keep off the rain.

On the way out of the front door of a villa the schoolchild might greet the porter, who sometimes would have a little lodge by the door (in fact, the more unfortunate porter would sometimes even be chained to the wall), and pat, or edge his way gingerly around the guard dog. Mosaics bearing the legend '*cave canem*', 'Beware of the dog', have been found, and there is no doubt that a dog is still one of the best burglar deterrents. Dogs were kept as pets, and there are charming illustrations, in a variety of media, from wall paintings to grave stelai, of puppies, lap-dogs and other small dogs sitting hopefully by the dinner table, curled up at their owner's feet, and otherwise happily settled into the family. Guard dogs would be a different matter.

The Roman house looked inwards, but in the façades there might be small shops to let, and on leaving his front door the child might have special friends among the tenants to greet, before setting off through the narrow streets, maybe passing on his way clients hurrying to greet his father – or his father making his way to *his* patron.

It is not the place here to examine the nature of the patron–client relationship that permeated Roman culture from legendary times up to the sack of Rome in the fifth century AD, except to note ways in which it affected the daily round. In the late Republic and the Empire, obligations were certainly not so exclusive, altruistic or effective as histories and self-image would wish to suggest, but the system was a fact of life, and of a morning it was expected of a client that he should pay his respects to his patron, and perhaps accompany him about his business, especially to places like the law courts or to the Forum for some politicking. Rather like the feudal system, though not exactly parallel, everybody was a client to somebody, with, in Imperial times, the Emperor at the top. On the whole, however, a citizen of rank could expect to receive callers, rather than set about paying respects to another. At such times the client could ask for help, e.g., with legal matters, receive monetary assistance or, if he were, say, an impoverished young poet living in a garret, like Martial, or youth-about-town like Encolpius in the *Satyricon*, try to wangle an invitation to dinner. Providing food was a patronal obligation – not always comfortably fulfilled, but even the chance of a rather nasty free meal was not one to be turned down.

The morning call was, therefore, an important part of the day. The client, perhaps after waiting on one of the benches still surviving outside some richer houses, would enter the house by the front door, often set into a fairly unprepossessing façade, and enter into a different world (Fig. 6, see p. 25). There might be a corridor leading to the *atrium*, or the door might open straight onto it. This was the most important and focal part of the house – an airy hall, two stories high, with a rectangular opening to the sky (the *compluvium*), through which rain could be collected in the pool underneath, sunk into the *atrium* floor (the *impluvium*) (Fig. 7, see p. 27). The grandeur of the materials, decoration and furnishings of the *atrium* would depend upon the status and pocket of the owner – we shall come back to these. The *atrium* led onto the *tablinum*, the master's study. This was actually an open room, open both to the *atrium* and to the

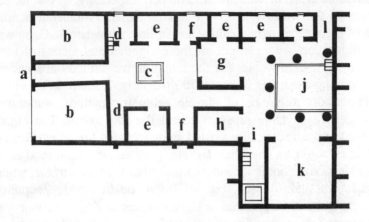

Figure 6. Ground plan of a villa, the House of the Tragic Poet, Pompeii. a = entrance, b = shops, c = *atrium*, d = staircase, e = bedrooms, f = *alae*, g = *tablinum*, h = *oecus*, i = kitchen, j = peristyle and *lararium*, k = *triclinium*, l = postern.

garden beyond, but it was the centre of authority. Here the patron would be seated, perhaps with his secretary (a male slave, very likely Greek) by his side. There might be shelves for scrolls, the family strong box (bolted to the floor to deter burglars, and securely locked – plenty of examples of Roman lock mechanisms and keys with teeth survive, working on just the same principles as the modern mortice [as opposed to cylinder] lock), his table, perhaps of marble (some fine examples survive), with finely moulded legs ending in animal claws, his chair inlaid with bronze or ivory, and around the walls portrait masks of distinguished ancestors. For those who lacked the necessary distinguished ancestors, such masks were a favourite motif in the later styles of wall paintings. The whole effect should have conspired to keep the client in his place – although in the case of a freedman and his former owner it could well happen that the freedman could afford richer surroundings: there was nothing to inhibit his gathering wealth and hoping that his sons could move up the ranking system.

On his way out, the client, frustrated or hopeful, might have more of an eye to his surroundings. Because of the devastating eruption of Pompeii and the silting up of the Tiber we are in the lucky position of having three Roman towns left to us in a remarkable state of intactness. Pompeii especially, gives us the homes of the wealthy and well-entertained; Herculaneum a mixture of the staggeringly wealthy and ordinary townsfolk; Ostia was a working port – we can put all these together and reconstruct the bustling jumble of Rome. For the moment, we can look at a variety of surviving examples of beautiful *atria* (Fig. 7, see p. 27).

The floors might be of simple geometric pattern, sometimes with decorative large mosaics round the *impluvium*. The highly detailed and exceptionally skilled floor mosaics for which Roman villas, even in provinces like Britain, are famous would tend to be found in 'living rooms' or sanctuaries rather than the *atrium*, where mosaic was indeed used, but tended to be in simple geometric patterns rather than pictorial designs (mosaic is also used as a wall decoration). One very famous example was certainly laid out in a dining-room, as amongst its devices are bits and pieces of debris from the dinner-table, as if waiting to be picked up by an alert pet, or cleared away by the slaves. Roman artists (i.e., artists working for Romans but most likely Greek) were very interested in naturalistic effects. They had good understanding of colour and light, so that they could convey the translucency of glass, or the bloom on a piece of fruit. They did not understand true perspective, but nonetheless were able to convey depth, both in terms, for example, of a painted pilaster seeming to stand out from the wall and of being able to give the impression of the room being opened out into a landscape beyond (particularly characteristic of 'Second Style'). All of these allowed artists and patrons to indulge their taste for *trompe l'oeil* effects, from mock-marbling to garden scenes to the elaborate theatrical fantasies of 'Fourth Style' painting.

Depending on the age of the property, our client might then be walking on haphazardly paved floor, almost like crazy paving, smooth marble, or mosaic. It is not something people are much given to speculating about, but one does wonder how often a leather-soled or hobnailed boot might have slithered on a well-kept floor.

The feeling around the client would be of space. The *atrium* was high – there is even a house in Herculaneum (the Samnite House) which has, unusually, a gallery running round the second floor. Suspended between the columns supporting the *compluvium*, in

Figure 7. An *atrium* with brazier, tables and *lararium*.

the types of *atrium* where these were found, there might be *oscilla*, decorated round plaques, moving gently in every hint of breeze. These could also be found as ornaments in the peristyle around the garden. There would also be a sense of sacredness, for the *atrium* was the ritual centre of the house.

There would often be a *lararium*, a shrine to the household gods, the Lares and Penates (though this might be found in another part of the house, e.g., the garden) (Fig. 7, see p. 27). This might take the form of a miniature temple, or perhaps something simpler, like a cupboard, containing the images of these protective deities. The master of the house would make sacrifices to them every day.

Here also would take place such ritual events as naming ceremonies for a baby, coming of age or wedding ceremonies. Large tables would be a normal feature of the furnishings, with zoomorphic (animal-shaped) table legs particularly favoured. Little tripod tables, often collapsible, were very common in Roman homes, and would be found used for many functions in the house – some have rings to hold bowls or cauldrons, some are what we would call occasional tables, useful by one's chair, or for holding an *objet d'art*. The *atrium* was a good place to show off a prized piece of statuary, or an Old Master Greek painting – collected as Old Masters would be collected today by those with the money, or opportunities of conquest. The Roman antiquarian making his way through the *cursus honorum* – the climb through the rankings of officialdom – would have plenty of chances to acquire such works of art while on suitable provincial postings.

Cicero, in his letters to his brother-in-law Atticus, urges him to send pieces from Greece, betraying a certain vulgarity in asking for suitable works to fit the rooms, rather than caring about the specific piece – rather like buying books for one's library for decorative purposes, rather than with the intention of loving and reading them.

Amongst the possibilities for the collector were actual removeable paintings – panel paintings. We tend to think of Greek and Roman painting as purely wall-painting, but portable pictures, and therefore art galleries, were also to be found.

The *tablinum* seems on the whole to have been open both to the *atrium* and the garden beyond, but there is at least one instance in Herculaneum of a house with wooden partitions (which indeed give it the name by which we know it) which could be slid open or closed on bronze tracks.

Usually, on either side of the *tablinum* would be an *ala*, or room-cum-passage, leading on to the peristyle, the colonnade surrounding the garden, off which would open various rooms – bedrooms, dining-rooms, and the garden itself.

We live in a society governed by time pressure and time aware-ness – bleeps on the radio, chiming clocks and beeping watches, even atomic clocks accurate to plus or minus a second in a million years. This is not a natural or a comfortable way to live, but so accustomed have we become to it that it is only in brief periods of holiday – usually away from home – that we can glimpse life lived in a world in which it is necessary only to have some idea of the time of day rather than the precise time. Perhaps the master of our household wished to be off to the law courts in good time. He might have a sundial to glance at in the garden, to give him a rough idea of how the morning was passing. The Romans took over the idea from the Greeks, and indeed began by taking over actual Greek sundials, which, of course, were not calibrated properly for a different latitude. They did, in time, overcome this unfortunate flaw, and the sundial principle was extended both to huge clocks, such as the one in the Campus Martius that used the shadow of an obelisk, or to minute pocket dials. I have seen a modern version of such a wrist or pocket sundial, manufactured in Brittany, and they do work rather well – in the appropriate latitude.

Otherwise, the man of substance might have a water-clock, which measures time against the water levels in a calibrated con-tainer. These could be set to give the time of day in each month, and were of quite adequate accuracy for Roman purposes. Small vessels working basically on the same principle as an hourglass were used, for example, for timing speeches in a law case, and they could be set for the occasion. For the larger devices it was necess-ary to vary the times according to the seasons, because the Roman day, although divided into twelve hours of day and twelve of night, varied in the length of the actual hours with the length of daylight, with the sixth hour (mid-day) as a constant. Many people would, however, continue to gauge the time of day from the position of the sun and, no doubt, from the state of their stomachs.

Before leaving to set about one's affairs, a visit to the latrine is always a good idea. Not every house was furnished with such a convenience (there were plenty of public toilets), but where they

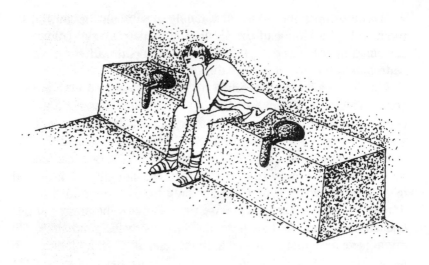

Figure 8.   Roman latrines.

did exist in private houses they tended to be placed close to the kitchens, for ease of plumbing. The same principle appears to have applied to private as to public latrines – the occupant sat over a hole leading down to continuous flushing water through to the sewers (Fig. 8). The materials for the seating could vary from wood in a military camp to rather splendid marble in decorated chambers with mosaic floors and carved armrests, the seats being ranked round the edges. The public toilets were rather convivial places (tunics provide more dignified coverage than modern trousers in such settings) – there is a gaming board scratched on the step by the toilets in Timgad so one could obviously expect to pass the time of day as well. They were also, if Martial is to be believed (XI.27), a good place to hang around hoping to pick up a dinner invitation. The question of separate provision for ladies and gentlemen does not receive much attention, but the evidence seems to be that there was none. The point about dignified coverage made above still applies. The Romans used sponges as toilet paper. In Housesteads fort on Hadrian's Wall the channel in front of the seats where one could wash one's individual sponge (applied on a stick) is still to be seen.

The toilet and the graffito appear to be inextricably linked in certain kinds of human consciousness, and Rome is no exception.

Even the privy in the house of a family of substance might not be exempt. In the House of the Gem at Herculaneum the Emperor's physician, no less, could not refrain from commenting on the facilities: 'Apollinaris, the doctor of the Emperor Titus, had a good crap here'.

One of the Romans most life-improving skills was water engineering. They understood hydraulics, and were able not only to transport water along aqueducts, which were magnificent examples of architecture as well as civil engineering, but they could deliver the water to the all-important baths, to individual streets or even (not always legally) to individual houses, for both household and ornamental use. Waste water, or water with waste, was then transported on through sewerage systems and, in Rome's case, emptied into the Tiber. The most famous of the city's sewers was the Cloaca Maxima, the point where it debouches into the Tiber being visible to this day.

The infrastructure of Rome itself in terms of such amenities could not attain the heights of efficiency of planned provincial towns, because it was older, more haphazardly built, and vastly bigger (estimated population under the Empire of a million, sizeable in modern terms, but staggeringly huge in ancient terms, and about eight square miles in area).

A familiar sight in the streets at any time of day, but especially of a morning, would be gatherings of women at the fountain-heads in the streets, collecting water for households without their own individual supply – and these would of course be the majority. Fountains and wells then and now in towns and villages without running water are excellent places to meet, gossip and make assignations. At home water could be drawn up from the cistern into which the *impluvium* drained, through a pillar-shaped wellhead. Many of these survive, with rope marks showing regular use.

Our schoolboy, creeping like a snail unwillingly, or ready to show off some newly-memorised verses, would doubtless have to squeeze past groups of women from the neighbouring *insulae* collecting their water – Roman towns were not strictly divided into desirable and undesirable, business and residential districts. A glance at a ground plan of a town like Pompeii will show the tight-packed promiscuous jumble of different grades of housing to be found in a Roman town. This is not to say that they lacked low-life areas – the bustling Suburra was notorious. The well-to-do,

31

Figure 9.   At the baker's.

middling, and poor lived cheek by jowl, or even quite literally on top of one another, as the higher one went in an *insula* the smaller, more uncomfortable, and indeed the more dangerous as fire-hazards the rooms, hence the poorer the occupants. There might be portable braziers in the upper rooms (a major cause of those fires), but cooking facilities, where they existed, would be limited and dangerous, so the occupants would go out to the bakers for fresh, warm bread, characteristically baked in a segmented round in a charcoal oven similar to the modern pizza-oven (Fig. 9), to the *thermopolium* for some wine, perhaps mulled, and a bite to eat: some cheese, nuts, cakes or fruit. Behind the counter, a charcoal stove would keep more substantial fare ready for the customer.

These fast-food shops, like many a Roman shop, were open-fronted, with a counter onto the street, and a painted sign advertising the shop's specialities. Doubtless the small child had to be restrained from the enticing sights and smells of the pastry shop after his eager morning visit. There is such a shop in a remarkable state of preservation at Herculaneum – Sextus Patulcus Felix's shop, with its various sizes of baking pan neatly hung on the walls, mixing bowls, supplies of wheat, and the mills to grind it (these were turned by asses whose remains have been left behind). Tutelary phallic symbols were found in the shop, as one might find a statue or picture of a saint in modern Italy.

Apart from the taverns, the wine shops with their jars set into the marble counters, and the *thermopolia*, there might not be a wide range of businesses to be seen on any one journey, though one certainly would not be able to ignore the ones that were there. The crowding and encroaching became so bad that Domitian had to decree a widening and tidying up of the pavements and alleys which, according to Martial, made walking the streets a much more pleasant experience – more space, less mud, and less risk of an involuntary encounter with the tools of a street barber's trade (VII.61). As in a modern souk or bazaar, Roman traders and craftsmen tended to be grouped together in specialist streets, so, for example, the Velabrum was the street of the cheesemongers, another street held the silversmiths, another the leatherworkers (a very smelly business – a tannery in the centre of town would not meet with much favour), and so on. Greengrocers, jewellers, butchers, carpenters, fish merchants, fullers – anyone with an eye to see could walk through the Roman streets and not be bored.

But school must be faced, alas. In order to master his letters, the child would work on the same materials as his father would for his correspondence – a hinged wooden base, with two or more sections, which could be closed for transportation, inlaid with wax, on which the letters would be incised using a stylus with a point at one end for writing and the other end flattened to erase mistakes. Paper did exist, made from the Egyptian papyrus plant, and carbonbased inks, with ingredients like soot or cuttlefish ink, but neither of these commodities has much chance of survival except in very specific conditions, such as the aridity of Egypt, and it was not easily come by – Cicero had to bale out Atticus with supplies of paper. In Britain, a 'paper' made of thin sheets of wood has been discovered. Parchment was also used.

The *litterator* would be watching the lesson closely, and the weight of his wrath might descend in a very literal sense upon the laggardly. Horace has left us with the memory of his basher of a schoolteacher, one Orbilius (*Epistles* II.1.69 ff.), and Martial complains not only about the schoolmaster's cruelty, but also about his wrecking the neighbours' slumbers with the noise of his shouting (VIII.48). On the other hand, Horace also gives us a gentler image of school – the teacher who coaxes his pupils to learn with the reward of something nice to eat (*Satires* I.1.25 f.). Learning by heart was an important part of the educational process – Rome still retained aspects of an oral culture: people read aloud even to themselves, and books and poetry were *listened to*.

Books were scrolls on rollers, made from lengths of papyrus glued together, and then an identifying tag was added to the roll. The *codex*, the shape of book with which we are familiar, did not come into use until the first century, and seems to have been very much the preserve of Christian literature. Its precursor was probably the *membranum* , a kind of vellum notepad. A man of means like Atticus could keep librarians well versed in the skills of making, looking after and labelling books. Reading these books was a laborious process, as one would continually need to be rolling up one end and unrolling the other – going back to check, scanning quickly for details, browsing, or looking forward to later passages were not very feasible – a different kind of reading was necessary. It could be argued that the necessity for the Roman to develop his memory, practise his aural skills, and follow carefully through in his reading actually gave him valuable mental equipment that is atrophied in the modern world and that one might wish we could regain, especially if one has any experience of teaching.

For the Roman wishing to get on in the world it was above all necessary to speak well, and while the youngster struggled with the basics, his older brother (assuming his family could afford a secondary education) would be studying with a rhetorician, from about the age of sixteen. The aim was to be able to speak well enough to sway one's hearers, no matter what the subject, and to this end stylistic devices and use of words were carefully studied, together with set cases to argue that tested the developing skills – books of these were produced. The obvious flaw in such a training, that the speaker could be plausible without personal conviction, exercised ancient minds, but is without the scope of this volume.

For the higher classes 'university' education would be sought in

Greece, at one of the philosophical schools in Athens. At all points Roman education was influenced by Greece – though without the Greek balance of music, intellectual and physical education.

Education for many a Roman child, of course, would mean learning a trade or craft, or household duties, so that the morning would be spent in the father's workshop, on the farm, in the kitchen, or indeed at play with pets, toy chariots, hobby horses, hoops, buckets and spades and pottery dolls.

Unless he were himself going down to the forum, accompanied by clients, or accompanying his own patron, the master of the house might have correspondence to see to – letters written by his own hand or dictated. Getting them delivered was not such an easy matter. He could despatch a slave, or, if the correspondence were going to someone posted abroad, be able to ask an official messenger to take it, but a letter from private citizen to private citizen might have to wait long enough until someone was going in the right direction and, seal or no seal, he might have to word his letter carefully in case of prying eyes. As Cicero's copious correspondence with his brother-in-law dates from the time of the convulsive death-throes of the Republic, he had pointedly to take this precaution on a regular basis.

With the morning's salutation and correspondence thus attended to, the master of our house would set out for the morning's affairs, perhaps, if he had no public business to attend to, he might visit the supervisor of his workshops. The Romans did not really have anything one could describe as a factory. Most production was in small workshops, but a kind of mass production (always dependent upon slave labour rather than mechanisation) was possible for commodities such as swords, terracotta lamps, or the hugely popular burnished red Arretine ware, known in Britain as Samian. Otherwise, a visit to one's bankers might be required, or to Ostia, to the warehouses, or the factors, with their trade advertised in mosaic in the pavements outside their offices. Reports on the production of wine or oil from country estates would be eagerly perused – Pliny fretted over bad seasons. And the owners of the *latifundia*, huge, and not always legally acquired, ranches that finished off the destruction of Italy's agricultural base after the ruin of the peasant classes as a result of the wars in the later Republican period, would read stock reports, or examine the quality of their leathers. Cows were more important for leather than meat or milk. Cheeses were made from goat's or sheep's milk as they commonly are in Italy today.

While all this bustle was going on, the leisured lady, having donned her overdress (*stola*), would be ready to seat herself in her chair (a famous relief from Trier shows a lady sitting in an elaborately woven high-backed wicker armchair at her toilette, surrounded by attendants), be made up, have her hair dressed and examine her jewellery (Fig. 5, see p. 21). Despite the obvious skill in making undergarments like the leather bikini bottom mentioned earlier, the Romans did not do much fine tailoring, and all their overgarments were very simple in shape, being variations on a theme of sewn-up rectangles, the breadth of the rectangle deciding whether the garment was sleeved (though sleeves were always short). A deciding factor in elegance would be the way the garment was caught up at the shoulders, with brooches, pins, or possibly stitching, creating either a very simple, or a pleasing slashed effect. The lower hem of the dress, covering the feet, would, for married women, often have a decorative border. The dress would be girdled under the bust in what we would call an Empire line – the early ninteenth century and 1960s style that was actually inspired by Classical originals. The basic shape of women's clothes did not change over centuries, with fashion variations rather in colour, textile (for those able to afford luxury garments) decoration and accessories.

The yarns used to produce these clothes would be spun by hand, using distaff and spindle, and mostly woven on upright looms. White was normal for men's tunics, but women tended to favour colours. As a raw material wool does, of course, already come in a range of attractive colours. Ovid, indeed, has advice for women on the colours that suit each type – blue, sea-green, saffron, amethyst purple, pink, different greys or browns – each of these has its excellent qualities for him (*Ars Amatoria*, III.170-92), but not royal purple, which is much too expensive. Natural dyestuffs included materials such as madder for red, saffron for yellow, wood-gall for black, lichens for soft greens. All of these are still used both for their subtlety and by those who dislike chemical dyes. Alum was used as a mordant (colour fixative) and sulphur as a bleaching agent. The most famous, luxurious and expensive dye of all was the royal purple mentioned above, which is obtained from the shellfish murex. It takes a lot of shellfish to produce a small amount of dye, and this sumptuous rich colour was reserved for really conspicuous consumption, or the distinguishing stripes on toga or tunic of which we shall hear more later.

Before being made up, cloth would be treated by the fullers, using processes any fuller of more recent years would still have recognised: bleaching with urine or soda, washing with fuller's earth, stretching to even it out, shrinking to size, carding, trimming and pressing. It was also the fuller's job to do the bleaching and later cleaning, using fuller's earth again, treading the clothes in a vat to dislodge the dirt, and then rinsing. A series of paintings from a fullery at Pompeii illustrates the process.

The perils of being an *ornatrix*, hair-dresser and make-up artist, we have already alluded to. Hairstyles did not become really outrageous until the Flavian period. Up until then, and sometimes afterwards, depending on fashion and the tastes of the influential and therefore copied, simpler styles, more akin to Greek hair-styles, with the hair parted in the middle and secured in a bun, perhaps held in place with a net or snood, and decorated with fillets, were more usual. Even after the fondness for wildly elabor-ate superstructures had abated somewhat, hair fashions could still be as complicated as any diadem that might be placed upon them.

Hair-lighteners were very popular, with inspiration drawn from the North, where the envied fair locks were more common. Bata-vian foam, Wiesbaden soap tablets and Mainz soap – a Gaulish invention of goat-fat and beechwood ash – are amongst the sub-stances mentioned. The last is apparently a good shampoo, but actually has no hair-lightening effect. Henna was known and used, but there is no mention of that other natural and safe highlighter, camomile.

After the hair comes the face. We are again indebted to the erotic poets and satirists for detail – Ovid's *Ars Amatoria* in par-ticular might have been written with the curiosity of the future social historian in mind. He even wrote a poem (only the beginning of which has survived, unfortunately) on the art of make-up (*Medicamina Faceiei Feminae*). There are archaeological treas-ures, like make-up boxes, full of little pots for the necessary ingredients, perfume flasks, perhaps in alabaster, or the exquisite

Roman glass (Fig. 5, see p. 21). All these would be laid out for morning use on the lady's dressing-table, together with such necessities as combs, tweezers, nail cleaners and mirrors of polished silver or bronze, or even lead-backed glass. They would all have to be packed up to be taken to the baths in the afternoon for reapplication.

Hair elsewhere on the body was not appreciated, and a variety of more or less frightening remedies was suggested. One that is unlikely to gain many modern fans was mentioned by Suetonius – running red-hot walnut shells over one's legs (*Augustus*, 68), though this may be a libel. Julius Caesar, he suggests, preferred tweezers, which were certainly much used (*Iulius*, 45). Otho apparently was depilated top to toe, and used a bread-poultice at least on his face (*Otho*, 12). Pumice stone was used as an abrasive depilatory, and Juvenal mentions the use of resin (VIII.115). Beyond these, some rather revolting concoctions, using blood, gall or powdered snake are to be found in Pliny (*Natural History*, XXVIII.249-55). Whatever methods were employed, it is amply clear from the references that not only women were particular in this regard.

The body would be attended to in the bath rather than at home. Ovid does warn against being seen about one's preparations, much as a modern agony aunt might. He does, however, recommend a face-pack first thing in the morning, and his poem on make-up offers a selection of recipes of varying degress of complexity, the easiest being crushed poppy seeds. Some ingredients, such as ground horn, ground seeds, cereals and honey were probably quite efficacious. White lead and natron are decidedly less appealing, and indeed positively harmful. One does also wonder whether an ingredient produced from birds' nests (process not described) was indeed an effective spot remover.

As to the actual face-painting, a moisturiser/foundation of grease from sheep's wool was common (let no modern woman scoff – we use the same thing and call it lanolin), but rather smelly it seems (*Ars Amatoria*, III.213-15). Face powders would be of a variety of more or less noxious substances such as the white lead or red natron mentioned above, ground lupin seeds or Illyrian irises. Rouge could be made from ochre or wine lees, and there are lots of references to products to darken the eyes. Suggested recipes include: from Pliny, bear's fat and lampblack mascara, also ants' eggs and squashed flies; from Ovid, eye-shadows of ash and saffron; from Juvenal, soot as eyebrow-darkener. Ovid even recommends beauty patches, and given the ravages some of the above could inflict, one is not surprised. Oddly, lips do not come in for the same attention, but one can well imagine that rouging agents could be used for lips as well as cheeks. All these substances would be applied by the skilled *ornatrix* using tiny spatulas.

Next comes a choice of jewellery, and here it has to be said that the skills of the goldsmiths and silversmiths of the ancient world were quite stunning – filigree, granulation, piercing, intricate ropes, repoussé work, lost wax casting, all these techniques were known and used. Inlay of precious stones, polished to give a cabochon effect rather than cut, was popular, and the Romans used semi-precious stones such as quartzes and garnets, as well as sapphires, aquamarines and emeralds from Egypt, often left in their natural crystal shape. Uncut diamonds are occasionally found, and, of course, that perennial favourite and most flattering of gems, the pearl.

The wearing of much jewellery was considered rather bad form, and Petronius satirises Trimalchio's gold-bedecked wife in the *Satyricon*. Snide comments about women wearing the family's wealth in their ears are also to be found in poetry – earrings were a favourite form of decoration, always of a pendant type. Bracelets, necklaces, diadems and hair ornaments were also worn (Fig. 5, see p. 21). Extremely common was the type of brooch known as the fibula – a kind of glorified safety-pin, found throughout the ancient world, from Greece to Celtic Britain. Finger rings could be decorative or functional. Betrothal rings were originally of iron, but iron set in gold, or pure gold became normal, and they were worn by the girl on the same finger as used today (a nerve was believed to travel from this finger to the heart). Charming late Roman gold rings have been found in Britain with a motif of clasped hands on the bezel. Gold rings were also worn by the *equites*, the knights, as a sign of their rank.

A dab of perfume always completes a toilette pleasantly, and phials of scents from the markets of the East, or Capua, would doubtless have their place in a cosmetics collection. The scents would be oil-based, and kept in glass flasks (pottery or metal perfume bottles are known, but it would keep better in glass). The Empress Poppaea, who had a brief and sordid reign with Nero, introduced a strong scent which thereafter was known by her name. (Perfume was also put into tombs as grave goods, and used in anointing corpses. Frankincense and myrrh have been identified, and a recipe including salt, cedar oil, honey, myrrh and balsam.)

Thus suitably accoutred, the mistress of the house would lock away, and perhaps even padlock, her treasures until it was time to go to the baths and, having wrapped herself in her cloak (*palla*), would be ready to visit friends, go to the temple or go shopping. The *palla* was more an overgrown shawl than a cloak, a rectangle which was wrapped about the body, making sure to cover the head, as it was not respectable for a woman's head to be uncovered. Only prostitutes wore togas.

Our lady might choose to be carried in a litter, so that her slaves would have the trouble of picking their way over the ruts worn in the paved streets by night-time wheeled traffic, and the drains (some streets in Pompeii have stepping stones across them, so the waste disposal, and even rain water disposal systems cannot always have been perfect). Litters could be quite a nuisance in the already crowded streets, which were mostly very narrow, and probably rather dark, where *insulae* several stories high rose up on either side. Apart from litters in which one might recline, shielded by curtains from the common gaze, there were also conveyances more like sedan chairs. Chariots, carts and wagons would not be seen at this time of day, as we have seen.

We should remember all the craftsmen who were necessary to maintain a culture of such high development – those who have left their records in the buildings and artefacts they created rather than in writing – the masons, carpenters, smiths, rope-makers, glass-blowers, leatherworkers, foundrymen, wheelwrights, potters, painters and all the others whose skills sustained and enhanced Roman life. We have information about craftsmen not only from their products, but also from excavated tools, from illustrations e.g., on wall-paintings or tombstone reliefs and in records such as official accounts of the price of materials. We know, for example, that carpenters had available to them high quality tools, some of which have a surprisingly modern look. Planes, adze-hammers, saw blades, chisels, dividers and gauges have all survived. No lathe has survived in fact or illustration, but they were clearly used for such purposes as turning table legs. The indefatigable Pliny (the Elder) advises on the best uses for particular woods, e.g., soft beech wood for chairs, tables and veneers. Many different varieties were used for practical and decorative effect. Pliny also mentions a craze for tables of citron wood from North Africa (XIII.96), which could fetch wild prices – Cicero paid a million sesterces for one. Supplies of it ran out by the end of the first century AD – not the least of Rome's depredations of the natural resources of North Africa, redounding to this day in the spread of the Sahara Desert.

Glass-working is interesting as an example of a commodity produced to an exceptional level of artistry, but at the same time capable of a Roman version of mass production, thanks to the first century BC invention of glass-blowing. Previously, glass had been moulded, molten or in rods, round a pre-formed core, ground from a block, or cast in moulds. The invention of a means of blowing the glass revolutionised the craft. Very few remains of glass furnaces of the Roman world have been found, and only one illustration, on a lamp from Dalmatia, showing a pot chamber for the glass to be heated to the correct temperature for blowing, and an annealing chamber above to allow it to cool gradually to prevent breakage. The basic ingredients are silica (sand), soda and lime, and it was important to find pure sand for high quality glass – sand from the Levant, the Italian shore near Cumae, Gaul and Spain, was prized.

The basic colour of the glass was a blueish-green, but the Roman craftsmen knew how to add minerals to provide a rich array of jewel colours. Decoration could be created in a mould, applied during the blowing process, or as plastic decoration in different or self colours, and by incision. Cameo cutting is most famously exemplified in the magnificent Portland Vase, which is still held in awe not only for its beauty, but by craftsmen for its virtuosity, and the Lycurgus Cup demonstrates relief carving of an extraordinary level of skill and artistry. Apart from vessels, delicate, chunky, plain or irridescent, works of genius and everyday ware, the Romans were also able to produce glass panes for windows. At Herculaneum, for example, there was a glazed picture window in one of the baths, and evidence for glazed-in peristyles, for example, at the Villa of the Papyrii. These would not, of course, be sheet glass but built up of small panes.

There is no space here to go into any depth of detail, but it is important to bear in mind the buzz of everyday life for the everyday Roman (now doubtless beginning to feel in need of a bite to eat) that lies in the background of the poetry of Vergil and Horace, the speeches of Cicero, the histories of Livy and the pronouncements of the great and, occasionally, good.

It has been a long morning. Time for lunch.

Afternoon

Having escaped from the torments of the classroom, the child would be eager for one of the two important functions of any child's existence – eating or play. Perhaps he or she would rush into the kitchen to coax something out of the cook, or maybe into the garden to play if lunch were not yet to be served. For the moderately well-off, such as our family, they would have their own garden: a grand affair in a villa, or a more humble courtyard behind the shop. An *insula* might have a garden court (Fig. 1, see p. 10), as at the House of the Paintings at Ostia, but the children of the poorer classes might have to amuse themselves in the street, or in the corner of the room, and contain their energies until they could go to the baths, or to exercise on the Campus Martius by the Tiber, the military training field where youngsters could receive physical training. Even in this crowded city the super-rich managed to have not only formal peristyle gardens but parkland as well. Nero, famously, created a beautiful park by (allegedly) burning down rather a lot of other people's homes. The normal villa garden, however, would be contained within the villa, rather than be without the actual building, as a modern garden is.

It has been possible to reconstruct some of the gardens at Pompeii and Herculaneum by using techniques such as pollen analysis and study of the remains of tree-roots to determine which plants were originally grown, as well as by using contemporary descriptions. The Romans were fond of gardens, and had a fine appreciation of natural beauty. Their gardens, used for practical as well as pleasurable purposes, were formal, but harmonious (Fig. 10, see p. 44). Decorative canals, or smaller channels, fountains, pools (Cicero is very scathing about rich folks with their fishponds – actually a coded reference to Lucullus, whose fishponds were particularly famous), statuary, trellis work and pergolas, trees and plants were elegantly combined. Apart from physical remains, there are also pictorial representations, such as the exquisite

43

Figure 10. Gardening for the rich – based on the Villa off the Papyri, Herculaneum.

frescos from the 'Garden Room' of Livia's villa at Prima Porta, one of the glories of Roman art, and other examples of garden scenes from villas of the less famous. The fashion for garden paintings, villa scenes and landscapes is said by the Elder Pliny to have been started by Spurius Tertius in the Augustan period (*Natural History*, XXXV.16). From Livia's room we seem to look out from a terrace with a hint of a canopy overhead, across a trellis fence to lawns and a decorative terrace wall beyond which we see bushes, flowers and fruit trees where birds perch, or are just about to alight, the foliage thick and stretching out and fading to blue in the distance. The impression is of a combination of formality and beautiful wildness, such as the Younger Pliny evokes when describing the view looking out from the orderly charms of his garden at his Tuscan villa, with its clipped box hedges, to the countryside beyond (*Letters*, V.6). Students of later European history may recognise that same combination of formal and Romantic that characterises the late eighteenth/early nineteenth century taste in these matters.

Fruits and herbs were grown for practical as well as decorative purposes. Pliny had hedges of box and rosemary, mulberry and fig trees, a vine-wrapped pergola and a kitchen garden at his place at Laurentium (*Letters*, II.17). An actual market garden has been excavated at Pompeii. Creepers like acanthus and ivy, trees like plane, laurel and cypress, fruit trees like pomegranate, citron, quince and damson, herbs such as chervil, coriander, fennel and parsley all had their place. The Roman garden was full of variety and scent, and the gardener understood how to make the best of different soils for pleasure and professional horticulture – a subject fit even for poetry (Vergil, *Georgics*, II). Roses, violets and hyacinths were known to have been favourite flowers, found, for example, at the House of the Vettii, Pompeii.

There could also be a shrine in the garden – from a simple niche to a sizeable temple, such as the Serapion at Hadrian's vast villa on the road between Rome and Tivoli. Quite commonly there would be an ithyphallic statue of Priapus, a Greek fertility god who was to the Romans a garden god.

Eating *al fresco* is one of the joys of living in a Mediterranean climate (mosquitoes permitting), and many a garden would have an outdoor *triclinium* (dining-room). This could range from a simple dining area, perhaps under an arbour, to the rustic fantasy in white marble and vine round a catch basin where some of the dishes were actually set to float, that Pliny created in the depths of his Tuscan garden. Even an indoor dining-room could be designed to open onto the gardens, and Pompeiian villas often have an *oecus*, a living room possibly used as a fair-weather dining-room. In the more luxurious and spacious houses there is not always necessarily a defined break between indoors and outdoors, but a delicious blending of the two. For the less-fortunate souls living in cramped, stifling, fire-trap rooms at the top of an *insula* there was not so much scope for the indulgences of Romantic design, one hardly need say, though the peckish child could doubtless divert him- or herself with a game of knucklebones as well as a more privileged peer, whilst waiting for something to be brought in from the *thermopolium* or cooked on a hazardous portable brazier.

Knucklebones was a favourite game of the Classical world, a variant of dice, made more interesting by the uneven shapes of the playing pieces. The highest score (all different numbers) was a Venus, the lowest (all the same) was a dog. In dice-playing on the other hand (Roman dice were cubes with the same number arrangement that we still use), the Venus was a score of three sixes. Three was the normal number of dice for board games. Either of these games could be played in a corner out of the way of the adults, though probably not for money, as adults would play them. Another favourite simple game still played in Italy today and known as *morra* (Latin *inicatio*) is a guessing game. The players have to raise a number of fingers on their right hand, and call out the total. The game goes on till someone guesses the right number. Augustus had a favourite, odds and evens (*par impar*), in which the trick was to guess the number of pebbles hidden in the players' hands. He played it for money, but sportingly provided his family with the gambling funds. Without that extra spice a youngster might have got bored quite quickly. There might also be the additional hazard of keeping the playing pieces out of the way of one's baby brother who might try to eat them once the joys of mastering the art of walking with the aid of his baby-walker had palled. A second century AD tomb painting in Rome shows a just-walking little boy with his walker – a wheeled frame, with a front spoke, also wheeled, for stability.

One can, of course, always divert oneself with a pet. Apart from dogs, often seen in relief, painting and mosaic, and even celebrated in verse (Martial, I.109) as companions or working dogs (for hunting or guarding), birds appear to have been particularly popular. Lesbia's pet sparrow (Catullus, 3) is the most famous of them all, but there are other references to birds, literary and pictorial. In one of his epigrams Martial gives a list of assorted pets, though the interest they inspire does not seem to be entirely innocent: lynx, dog, monkey, mongoose, magpie, snake and nightingale (VII.87). This does in fact seem to be a fair representation of the variety of Roman pets. There is another unusual pet in a relief of a dinner party scene in which, instead of the usual dog looking on hopefully, a small chubby pig stands by the couch. The cat on the whole is wild, rather than domesticated. Though there is, for example, a painting from Pompeii of a well-fed, and very domesticated-looking, moggy comfortably settled in charge of a footstool. A touching grave stele from the south of France shows a young girl with a hen (perhaps also a pet) at her feet, clutching her kitten against her chest, hands around its stomach, as children do. Whether mice were kept as pets, or just captured for the occasion is not clear, but Horace does refer to a children's game of harnessing mice to little carts (*Satires*, II.3.249).

The portrayal of wild or domesticated animals in art often reveals a great affection and sensitivity, but the other side of the Roman character should not be forgotten. Alongside all these charming images go the darker visions of the hunt, one of many a Roman's great country pleasures, which is at least not wholly unnatural – they did eat game when they could – and worse, the revolting barbarities of the games. A culture which could embrace gladiatorial contests and plays in which people were tortured to death for real was not one that was going to have kindness to animals and conservation of exotic species at the top of its list of concerns. Quite on the contrary, in fact, as the wild beast hunts and slaughter in the arena and the search for obscure delicacies to excite jaded palates show us. As well as destroying the indigenous plant cover in North Africa in order to maximise grain supply to Rome (and thereby starting an inexorable process of desertification) their taste for watching unusual animals being butchered wiped out several animal populations of lions, tigers, hippopotami and elephants in Northern Africa and the Middle East. This too was a part of Roman everyday realities.

Now, however, if the stomach has settled, it is the fifth hour, and time to think of lunch. The unfortunate citizens of Pompeii and Herculaneum had their plans for lunch dramatically, and for some, permanently, interrupted. The priests of Isis were settling down to eggs, nuts and lentils – all beautifully preserved. A young lad lying ill in his room at Herculaneum was having chicken. Lunch was not the main meal of the day and would be fairly simple – wheaten or barley bread (barley certainly for the slave and the poor), meat or fish, vegetables, fruit and cheeses would be normal. Marcus Aurelius (later than our period, but such things do not change much) describes a simple lunch in the country – bread, beans, onions and herrings with their roe (*Letters*, IV.6). Olives, figs and salads were popular in ancient as in modern Italy. Those who frequented the wine-bars were doubtless less than pleased with Nero when he issued an edict restricting the fast-food on sale there to green vegetables and dried beans (Suetonius, *Nero*, 16) – one of a series of attempts by the Julio–Claudian emperors to limit consumption and expenditure by means of sumptuary laws. (Though, as a rule, the patrons of the taverns and the hot-food shops would not be amongst Rome's big spenders.) The sumptuary laws were, of course, as successful as all such laws always are in the end – it is no more possible to legislate to make people frugal than it is to legislate to make them good.

Water, honey-water or diluted wine would help to wash lunch down. Broths and pottages based on beans, barley or spelt were highly enough regarded to have their place in Apicius' cookery book, that great treasure of the social historian and foodie, and are cheap and nutritious. Cereal-based gruels and porridges formed the basic food at least of the peasant populations of the Mediterranean area for thousands of years, ante-dating the development of bread as the staff of life. Modern dishes like polenta, bulgur, couscous or risotto are their descendants. Such dishes would certainly feature on dinner menus, as their inclusion in Apicius' book shows, but they may also have perked up a working man's lunch on a dreary winter's day – perhaps even transported to workshop or field in a 'vacuum flask'. This is not actually as fanciful as it sounds. The Romans understood the principles of insulation, and a rather fine bronze and iron vessel, working on the same principle as the modern vacuum flask, with an inner and outer shell, insulated by air, has been found at Pompeii.

The sixth hour, Martial tells us, is siesta-time. Not only is a siesta both sensible and pleasurable in the summer's stifling heat in Rome, but as the afternoon would be devoted to exercise and bathing (or the excitements of the races or the games) it would be a healthy precaution, even after the fairly light meal the Romans had for lunch.

For the less-privileged, on the top floor of a crowded *insula*, there would be little comfort to be gained, and the escape to the baths must have been a real relief. For the wealthy, this leisure hour would have been considerably more agreeable. Indeed, were one at one's place in the country, or by the sea, say on the Campanian coast, there could well be a choice of rooms designed specifically for the moment – to catch the sea breezes in summer, or warmed by the furnace-house and away from household clamour in the winter. These opulent, and sometimes enormous, establishments, where the rich could indulge themselves and expand away from the crush of Rome, had apartments designed to suit the time of day and the time of year.

Of course, siesta-time was also a good opportunity for a little amorous dalliance. The light filtering through the shutters, as if through trees, like the soft light of dusk and dawn, is approvingly noted by Ovid (*Amores*, I.5) as an encouragement to the bashful girl – she would not manage to retain her bashfulness long in his company, shade or no shade. Catullus also makes a tryst for siesta time (32), although in his rather less delicately worded case, it is clear he would be happy not to wait.

And so to the baths (Fig. 11, see p. 50). It would be hard to overestimate the importance of the baths in the everyday lives of Romans of all classes. They were places to do a great deal more than simply divest oneself of dirt – they functioned as social clubs, gymnasia, public libraries, auditoria – even art galleries. A Roman man or woman could spend a sizeable part of the afternoon there, because there was plenty going on. It might even be suggested that we should add a third to the famous two demands for the pacification of the Roman mob: bread and circuses. Bread represents the corn dole to keep the potentially-disaffected urban poor fed, circuses the various games provided partly as ceremonial duty, partly as self-advertisement by the magisterial classes to keep them entertained – and there were many days of public holiday to fill (over 150 days in the year). The third amenity is the baths, to keep them clean, also to entertain, to provide somewhere beautiful, spacious, luxurious and warm for everybody's benefit. Again the building of such institutions, that we would regard as the responsibility of public authority, would be financed by the not entirely altruistic generosity of the rich and ambitious. (It must be remembered that to be ambitious, to be *seen* to be ambitious and to be self-promoting were regarded as positive qualities in the ancient world. The modern, certainly British, convention of self-deprecation, either genuine or disingenuous, would be as alien to a Roman as their apparently shameless self-congratulation seems to us.)

There is a parallel, very close in many ways to the Roman baths, in the *hamam*, the Turkish baths of the Middle East, which are very different from the steamy claustrophobia thought of as Turkish baths elsewhere. As with Rome, the buildings range from functional little local establishments to grand and beautiful archi-

Figure 11.   At the baths – the *caldarium*.

tectural masterpieces – though even the splendour of the Otto-
mans produced nothing on the scale of some Roman baths. The
ruins of part of the third century AD Baths of Caracalla in Rome
itself, for example, now comfortably accommodate the largest
stage in the world. As with Rome, the *hamam* is a place to go with
friends, spend hours in the leisurely process of bathing, being
massaged, sipping a refreshing drink. The processes are similar: a
hot room (not steam-filled, but heated to a point where water
simply evaporates) to open the pores, cleansing, a massage and
then a bracing splash with cold water, after which it is necessary to
rest for a while. The Roman processes, as we shall see, were
somewhat more complicated, but along the same principles, and
the end result would be the same: one emerges feeling cleaner
than anyone who has only experienced the ordinary modern bath
or shower could imagine, and relaxed and energised at the same

time. The Romans were on to a good thing here, and what is remarkable about the baths is that this is one pleasure that they most certainly did not keep for the lucky few – the baths were open to everyone for a deliberately tiny fee, and free for children.

The lucky few might have their own private baths at home, but probably did not make use of them as often as the public ones. They were fired up for guests; bathing could be as much of a party activity as a good dinner (e.g., Cicero, *Letters to Atticus*, II.3).

Baths were open to both men and women, and while some baths show separate provision for the sexes (the women's baths being more cramped than the men's next door – e.g., the Forum Baths, or the Stabian Baths, at Pompeii; interestingly, it appears that women preferred their baths hotter than the men – at the Forum Baths in Herculaneum the women's section had a separate furnace, and more hot-air pipes), there was certainly the possibility of mixed bathing at the large *thermae* up until the time of Hadrian, who decided that the opportunities for scandal were too great and too often taken. There were more modest, in every sense, local *balneae* to cater for women who did not care for this, and it has been suggested that when new baths were built the older ones would be relegated to women's use. (A women's bath might be the one place one could find ladies-only latrines, if there were any who regarded this as a problem.) Otherwise segregation was by time rather than place – after Hadrian's intervention men could only go to the baths after the eighth hour. There is again a parallel with the *hamam*. There was a time when mixed bathing did take place (utterly unthinkable in this century at the least), the more grandiose may have separate provision for men and women, otherwise men and women bathe in the same rooms on different days.

The first stop on entering the baths would be the *apodyterium*, where one undressed and left one's clothes folded on a shelf, with or without separate segments, under the care of either an attendant, or one's own slave. This was a necessary precaution, as theft of clothes from the *apodyterium* was quite a common crime, and there was a thriving trade in second-hand clothes. A few wretched souls caught in the Herculaneum Forum Baths tried to save themselves by climbing on to the clothes shelves to avoid the boiling volcanic mud – their skeletons were found there. Basins for washing hands and feet were also provided here.

The head of our household would probably have had his own slaves with him, his masseur, towel carrier etc., who would not only be familiar with his needs and whims, but cheaper than shelling out for all the various services provided by the management of the baths. His wife would need her handmaidens and *ornatrix*, for she would not only have to be attended throughout her bath, but restored to coiffed and painted glory afterwards.

The bather could move by graduated stages through the heating and cooling processes: rather than just one hot room, Roman baths provided a warm room (*tepidarium*), and hot room (*caldarium*), and even, if desired, a sweat room (*sudatorium*). These were heated by the same kind of underfloor heating (the furnace-heated hypocaust) that the Romans used for domestic central heating, the heat being trasmitted by radiation under floors raised on pillars, and also along walls, through hot air pipes. Hot water boilers were also sometimes used. (Domestic central heating was, of course, commoner in the Northern parts of the Empire.) The flow of water, hot or cold, was controlled by valve systems. Wherever hot springs were to be found, the Romans were glad to exploit them, recognising the therapeutic as well as recreational opportunities. The volcanic area around Vesuvius, for example, carried its benefits in hot springs and rich soils, as well as its fearful hazards. Sea water baths were also appreciated. Cooling off would be in a swimming pool.

There is, however, little point in bathing *before* taking exercise, and the baths were also often well-appointed health clubs. An exercise ground, a *palaestra*, would be a normal adjunct to any sizeable establishment. A variety of games would be played here, both by men and by women. Roman girls were not subjected to the rigours of training expected of Spartan girls, nor were they kept in seclusion like Athenian girls. They were able to enjoy, for example, a game of ball, just as their brothers were, should their tastes so incline. People being what they are, Rome had its share of tomboys, as well as those simply acknowledging the enjoyment and good sense of *mens sana in corpore sano* (a healthy mind in a healthy body). There are even reports of women gladiators. Juvenal satirises girls who practise sword-play against wooden practice-targets, and who perhaps dream of the arena (VI.246 ff.). That might strike the modern reader as a pretty strange dream –

it is hard to imagine wanting to be part of the bill of fare in such a place. For a slave, however, to be chosen for the gladiatorial schools could be more than just another kind of degradation. Those who managed not only to survive but also to capture the crowd's lasting fancy could achieve glory, fortune, even freedom, just as a boxer nowadays might rise from humble circumstances to being a media darling. The difference is, of course, that we stop fights as soon as an injury causes concern, and if a boxer dies it is an occasion of sorrow, scandal and enquiry – not the whole point of the exercise (the gladiatorial games were the development of funerary ritual and blood sacrifice, the religious rite still providing an increasingly hollow excuse). Yet there are always those, women as well as men, for whom danger, adrenalin, even blood give their lives a heady charge of excitement. This is as true of the innocence of, say, rock climbing as of the sweaty thrills of the arena, sword in hand and the roar of the crowd in one's ears.

Even taking healthy exercise would not, alas, be enough to ensure a long life for the Roman girl. The average life expectancy for a woman has been calculated as 27 years – largely as a result of the perils of child-bearing. The case histories of doctors of the Classical period make for grim reading. Gynaecological knowledge was in some ways quite advanced – doctors did understand internal anatomy to some extent. Among the medical instruments of Roman times that have been found are examples of vaginal and anal specula. They look painful, but beautifully engineered (women who wince at these may be gratified by the reaction of men to the equally beautifully engineered human castrators that have also survived. Juvenal notes the advantages perceived by women that the action of these instruments conferred – no scratchy beards and no abortions [VI.366 ff.].)

Knowledge of conception and therefore contraception was a mixture of the factual and effective, and the fanciful – but they had no means of knowing which was which. Without an adequate understanding of infection, doctors were frequently reduced to observation rather than intervention – they were more successful surgeons than physicians. In this context it is particularly relevant to puerperal fever, clearly a major killer. We shall look again at some of these matters in the final section of the book. Let us simply raise the question here whether the reported self-indulgence and hedonism of the upper-class women of the Late Republic and in the Empire did not have a deep fear underlying it and a sense of limited time. A reluctance to bear children – to the extent that Augustus had to bring in legislation to try to promote it – may not just have been selfishness, or even the effects of lead-poisoning from the water-pipes, which has been given the blame. Whatever the strict Republican ideals may have been, the Roman mother had no need to be tied down by rearing, playing with, educating or even feeding her child, but she could not delegate the responsibility, and therefore the risk, of bearing it. The girl bashing away at a target with her sword, the girl lingering in the portico to arrange a tryst with her lover, the girl flirting at the races – all of these were surely aware that their chances of living to a ripe old age in the bosom of their families were not too good. It has been suggested that an average marriage might last 10-15 years. Men too were susceptible to illness, and there was an abundance of unnatural causes of death – foreign and domestic misadventure. Added to this was the fact that upper-class girls married husbands much older than themselves. Their youth increased their own physical hazards, but they did stand to gain a pleasantly independent life as a widow *if* they survived. Lengthy marriages were fêted not so much as a victory for conjugal love as an avoidance of fatal accident.

Let us not, however, spoil the pleasure of the day and instead return to the *palaestra*. Military skills often form the basis of sporting skills, and this was as true for the Romans as any culture. Cavalry training and route-marching would have no place in the recreational surroundings of the baths, but running, jumping, swimming, spear-throwing, archery, wrestling and the like, all still part of our sporting canon, would be the exercise of civilians as much as of soldiers. Wrestling, which despite being an Olympic sport has a somewhat down-market image nowadays, was an honourable and very popular sport. Our young schoolboy can easily be imagined diving into a scrap. For a proper match the contestants would strip, oil themselves for suppleness, and then cover the oil with dust, to prevent cheating by slithering out of the opponent's grasp.

Weight-lifting was enjoyed by women as well as men. Juvenal refers to women rushing to the masseur after lifting weights

(VI.422 -3), and there are also references in Martial. One is bound to wonder which was regarded as the greater pleasure.

There was a whole range of different ball-games, with balls of varying composition: the *pila*, a small handball; the *paganica*, a feather-stuffed handball; the *follis*, an inflated ball which could be used for games a little like volleyball, in which players punched the ball at each other; the *harpastum*, stuffed with sand, was used in a game not unlike rugby in which one had to grab the ball and watch out for shoving, feinting and sprinting. *Trigon* was played with a *pila*. In this game there were three players standing at the points of a triangle and throwing the ball amongst each other at random. The aim was to throw with one hand and catch with another. In the *cena Trimalchionis* (the most famous episode of the *Satyricon*), Petronius' hero watches an elderly man, who turns out to be Trimalchio, playing this game at the baths with some beautiful youths (who particularly caught his eye), but disdaining to pick up the balls that fell, instead being resupplied from a bag carried by a slave (27). The object, of course, was *not* to let the ball fall. Handball was so popular that the larger household might even run to a special room, the *sphaeristerium*, designed for it. There is a huge array of possible games to be played with the simple aid of a ball, and the Romans had plenty, such as variants of games like *pelota* or the Eton Wall Game.

Good ideas work, and the simplest of games or toys can pass virtually unchanged down the centuries. Another favourite among women was the hoop (*trochus*), which was propelled and guided with a hooked stick called a key. A mediaeval, Victorian or twentieth century child might be found playing exactly the same game.

While one had to strip to prepare to wrestle, nudity for sport was considered bad form by the Romans. Instead they wore yet another form of the basic dress of tunic to exercise in. Martial does refer to a form of leggings worn by women (VII.67) or, in the same poem, a cloak to wear whilst playing ball on a cold day. This resistence to nudity was not the only difference between the Romans and the Greeks, their mentors in so many things. The pursuit of the ideal, the perfection of physical beauty, athletic excellence as part of the goal of the educated man, these did not strike chords in rougher Roman hearts. They recognised the utility of exercise – *mens sana in corpore sano* – but had no cult of the body. Martial physical training was carried out each day in the Campus Martius by civilians as well as soldiers, and here one would find young men practising some of the skills mentioned above that would not be suitable in the *palaestra* at the baths. These were considered manly, and, for a people almost constantly involved in the process of conquest and colonisation, appropriate, but the pursuit of physical perfection was not for them a goal worthy in itself.

After their exercise, mother, father and offspring would be all too ready for the pleasures of the bath, some basic body maintenance like depilation, a massage, and the other relaxing delights of the establishment.

The first step then, after a good work-out, or a little desultory ball-throwing, was the *tepidarium* to start the pore-opening, deep-cleansing process. For soap, the Romans used the ubiquitous and vital olive oil. This was smeared on to the body, and cleaned off after the sweating and splashing process, with a scraper-like implement called a *strigil* It may sound messy, but this is actually a very effective way of getting clean, especially when combined with the processes of increasing warmth – anyone who has had a genuine Turkish bath will know that, after a time spent sweating and soaping, the scurf can be scrubbed off what one had originally imagined to be a normally-clean body in an astonishing way.

The *tepidarium* would be provided with benches round the walls – of marble in a reasonably luxurious bath house, with shelves for towels or wraps – and the floors would be decorated with mosaic, in a plain geometric pattern, or something rather more sumptuous. The *tepidarium* of the Forum baths at Herculaneum, for example, was resplendent with a mosaic of a Triton with serpent legs (a popular motif), and dolphins – an appropriately watery theme for the setting. Here the master of our household would again be available for the attentions of his clients. He may have gone to the baths with some of them, in the same way that they would accompany him about his public business, in order to demonstrate his prestige and ensure support. Others, clients or hopefuls, may have chosen to coincide on bathing day (for the whole elaborate procedure would not necessarily take place every day) in an attempt to secure an invitation to dinner – just as Encolpius does from Trimalchio.

The rest of the process followed an optional pattern. In the *caldarium*, the hot room, there might be a basin with cold water for splashing on the face to relieve the heat, and there would be a hot water bath for water to sprinkle or pour onto the sweating body (just as in a *hamam*), perhaps even to immerse the body in (Fig. 11, see p. 50). The bather might also use the *sudatorium* – the sweat room, or 'dry bath', which was more like a sauna. The *caldarium* might be omitted, and a quick bather could go straight from *sudatorium* to cold plunge, in the more brutal Scandinavian method. While the sweating was going on, so would the scraping process, with the *strigil* This is obviously not particularly easy to do for oneself, and here the services of one's slave would be required. The poorer bather would have to pay for the services of an attendant. Even given the low price of admission that might, however, be too much for some so that they were reduced to rubbing themselves against the marble walls. The Emperor Hadrian is reported to have been so moved by the sight of an old soldier doing this that he gave him money and slaves. A friend could, of course, also help.

The hot room need not necesarily be a claustrophobic place, despite the heat and bodies. The Suburban Baths at Herculaneum, for example, had a large glazed window at one end looking out over the sea – a relaxing and cooling view to temper the heat of the room. Skylights were a common light source.

The bathing is completed with a cold plunge in the *frigidarium.* This has very beneficial effects, closing the pores and refreshing and revitalising a body rendered limp in the heat. Interestingly, we can see from the Herculaneum Forum Baths that not only did the women who patronised these baths like their hot room hotter, as demonstrated by the separate furnace and greater number of hot-air pipes already mentioned (liking one's bath hot was a sign of effeminacy), but also they drew the line at a cold plunge – there is no *frigidarium* in their section. (Elsewhere, curiously, there are reports of women's baths at *lower* temperatures than those of the men.)

Here would be a good place for women to attend to the business of making themselves beautiful with the face-packs and the like that Ovid warned them to keep hidden. But not, even so, that hidden – Martial is unkind enough to pillory one Thaïs, who entered the baths covered in a green depilatory, and with a mask of chalk, vinegar and bean-paste, and all because her own natural smell, he says, was even worse (VI.93). Did he see, or was he told? Surely even the tarts who favoured mixed bathing establishments drew the line at exposing their preparations to potential clients? Various handicraft tools have been found at the extensive and rather fine baths at the military town of Caerleon (Isca) in Wales, suggesting that the baths were a good place to combine a little gossip and one's sewing in comfort. The bathers would not always be naked. A shift, or a towel might be worn.

Interestingly, among the accoutrements of the *frigidarium* of the Forum Baths at Herculaneum are bronze candelabra, not only for the shorter days of winter, but for the evening. In Rome, the rule in Republican times was that the baths closed at sunset, though they stayed open later under the Empire. For those without luxurious homes to go to, there would indeed be every temptation to stay and enjoy the various pleasures the baths offered for as long as possible. For, after one had been appropriately rubbed, slapped and pummelled by a trained masseur (even women were attended by male slaves and masseurs, so Martial and Juvenal tell us), there were indeed pleasures available which had nothing to do with the mundane chore of cleaning oneself.

The determinedly mundane, or indeed the seeker after novelty, might even avoid a prolonged visit either to a private bathhouse or a public establishment. According to the Elder Pliny, one Sergius Orata (2nd-1st centuries BC) is credited with the invention of the shower bath, from which he apparently derived much profit, adding them as the latest modern convenience to the country houses he sold (*Natural History*, IX.79). (He also invented oyster ponds, at the fashionable Campanian coastal resort of Baiae, which shows he knew a thing or two about pleasing Roman tastes. Baiae was one of the places whither the smart set repaired to escape the torrid miseries of summer in the city, and indulge in the Roman equivalents of huntin', shootin' and fishin' [i.e., the same thing without firearms], go sailing – Catullus even wrote a poem about his yacht [4] – indulge their architectural fancies, get down to one's books or writing away from the demands of the capital, for those whose tastes ran that way, and entertain friends.)

After all that exercise, sweating, a bracing cold plunge and pummelling, one would be in need of a rest (actually a necessity, as the process leaves one feeling quite weak – the well-appointed *hamam* provides somewhere to lie down and recover), something to drink and perhaps a bite to eat. Some prepared food was actually on sale in the baths, and remains of cups and 'finger food', like chicken legs, pig and sheep bones, and shellfish, either bought on the spot or taken as a picnic, are among the interesting finds from Caerleon. Doubtless neighbouring taverns also did a roaring trade.

As the bathers don their clothes again, retrieving them from the bath attendant or personal slave, the divisions of rank that could hardly be discerned in a mass of flushed sweaty bodies would become visible. In the case of women, elegance of manufacture and richness of material would be the telling factors, but with men there were uniforms of rank.

While his mother was suitably re-arranged at the hands of her *ornatrix* and other maids, and his sister dried off and dressed in her turn, our schoolboy would be pulling on his tunic again (Fig. 2, see p. 15) and over it, assuming he was formally dressed for the occasion, his toga . Up until the time of his coming-of-age (at about fifteen or sixteen years old), the boy would wear the *toga praetexta*, that is, a toga edged with a purple stripe. On coming of age, he would put this away, and assume the *toga virilis* (Fig. 2, see p. 15), the toga of manhood, which was pure white (and keeping it that way would cost him plenty in laundry fees – imagine a clumsy white wool wraparound in the dirty, dusty streets of a Mediterranean town).

We have not yet placed precisely the master of our chosen household. He is not of the highest rank, but he has the money qualification (400,000 sesterces) to be one of the second rank – an *eques* (knight – the name derives from the very early qualification of cavalrymen able to provide their own horses). He is able to demonstrate his position in society by the wearing of a gold ring, as we have seen, and, more immediately visibly, by wearing a white tunic with a *narrow* purple stripe (the *angustus clavus*) down the back and front. To be a citizen of the second rank was by no means to be what we would think of as a second-class citizen – the *equites* and the senatorial class intermingled freely.

The senatorial class was, however, right at the top of the tree, and a senator was distinguished by his tunic, which had a *broad* purple stripe (the *latus clavus*) front and back, by his toga, because the senator took up once again the purple-bordered *toga praetexta*, and by the crescent embroidered or appliquéd to the upper of his shoes. The magistrate wore a shoe with a higher sole than the ordinary senator, but both had the crescent. A variety of shoes has survived in Northern Europe, on sites where water-logged conditions favour the preservation of leather, ranging from delicately-laced sandals to hob-nailed boots (Fig. 2, see p. 15). The shoemakers were expert in cutting the basic shoe all in one piece, needing only one seam up the heel. There was cut-out decoration, sometimes very intricate. Light sandals were only worn in the home and the more substantial laced shoe or boot was normal wear in the streets. One example of a shoe very similar in shape to the modern desert boot was found in London, but most examples tend to have more open lacing.

The length of the tunic also held an implication of status. The gentleman at home, or the tradesman of substance might wear a long tunic nearly to his ankles, the soldier's or slave's would be short (for, apart from anything else, simple practicality), and the striped tunic of the knight or senator slightly longer again.

This kind of visible stratification is one of the oddities that is striking in Roman society – here was a city that ruled most of the known world, and yet even amongst its freeborn citizens at home in that city there were messages of division rather than unity. The magistrates making their way about town made people well aware of their presence too. There were no discreet little signs, such as we might have, i.e., a fluttering pennant on an official car – the magistrates were preceded by their *lictors*, carrying the *fasces* (a bundle of rods representing their authority, and also an axe if the authority included right of life and death), who cleared passers-by unceremoniously out of the way, and added to the difficulties of getting about the crowded streets. Cicero, in fact, when he was on the run through Italy in some of his most insecure moments during Julius Caesar's march to power, found his *lictors* a real embarrass-ment to flight. A modern parallel might be found in the Soviet Union, where the enormous black Zil cars, used only by senior officials, would flash about their business with cheerful disregard for speed limits or the safety of pedestrians and other road users – a very unmistakeable sign of power.

Having dressed, whatever his rank, the bather might wish to

indulge in some restful entertainment. There were libraries at the big *thermae*, such as the Baths of Caracalla, and comfortable halls to sit and stroll in. There were rooms suitable for recitals of music or word. One of the pleasures – or hazards – of Roman social life was listening to the works of a hopeful poet, or writer of other genres (remember that one would also *listen* to a sober historical text-book, or forensic speech polished up for publication). Horace is amongst those who complain about this Roman version of vanity publishing (*Satires*, I.4.74 ff.). There were also galleries of statuary to enjoy.

Even at establishments less massive and magnificent than the great *thermae* of Rome, people obviously stayed on to be diverted. At the Suburban Baths in Herculaneum (where the room for resting after the baths had windows looking out over the sea and the harbour, soothing heart as well as body), there is a room which was obviously dedicated to less relaxed pleasures – if the graffiti on the walls are anything to go by. These include a list of the *offellae* (the sort of dishes provided by hot food shops) consumed; the amount spent on the girls; a paean to one Primigenia, evidently a courtesan of the highest quality much famed in the Pompeii area (or so the writing on local walls tells us); and even some words on the sexual dalliance of two men who appear to be servants of the Imperial household, Apelles and his 'brother' Dexter (the reference is to homosexual rather than familial relationship).

But let us return to gentler pursuits. What better way to idle away one's time before returning home to dinner than with a game or two. There is no culture in the world without games, and it is remarkable how the same kinds of 'board' games are to be found across the globe. Games with rules similar to Nine Men's Morris, Draughts, Backgammon turn up from the Viking North to the Pacific Islands. Rome was no exception. Remains of the favourites have been found across the Empire from the Mediterranean to Hadrian's Wall.

A great favourite was *duodecim scripta*, a racing game played along three rows of twelve places, each divided at the halfway point by a marker. Boards for this are found across the Empire, along with playing pieces of glass, bone and remodelled pieces of tile or chalk, plain or carved. There were, in the developed game, 15 pieces per side, and three dice. A board found at Ostia marked out with letters for the places, shows that it was played up the middle, down one side, and then down the third line, the object being to get all your pieces out (and, of course, impede your opponent). A version of the same game, *tabula* (mediaeval 'tables'), was reputedly a particular favourite of the Emperor Claudius. The use of letters evidently provided a game in itself, for there are examples of six letter words being used, each line making a sensible phrase, such as the one carved near a theatre in Rome:

CIRCUS * PLENUS
(the circus is full)
CLAMOR * INGENS
(there's a great din)
IANUAE * TECTAE
(the doors are shut)

Variations on the game have only two rows (like modern backgammon).

For the more tired mind, a Roman version of noughts and crosses (with diagonal lines across nine squares) might be less taxing. This was called *terni lapilli*.

Figure 12. Game-players

A huge favourite, with many boards and counters surviving particularly from the Northern Empire, was *ludus latrunculorum* (Fig. 12). This was a strategy game very similar in technique to the

Japanese game, *Go*. The pieces were lined up across a chequered board and were able to move like rooks in chess, up and down and across. Pieces could be captured, as in *Go*, by being sandwiched between two of the opponent's, so that it was important not to leave pieces isolated and vulnerable. There were boards of wood and stone, and the game was so popular that the pattern might be scratched on any convenient surface.

The gamesters would, of course, be seated. Pictorial evidence, and surviving examples (or surviving bits) show us a range of chairs, from the rough-hewn four-square high-backed sort that might appear in any peasant kitchen to this day, to elegant stools and backed chairs. Portability seems to have been a prized quality. As well as the folding tables mentioned in the chapter on Morning, there were folding stools, with leather seats (Fig. 5, see p. 21). A double U-shaped cross-section (straight and upturned on top of one another) was particularly favoured in the legs. More solid chairs, sometimes with a rounded back, also have the double U-shape to the legs. High-backed chairs, with and without arms, or the hint of a rounding-off from back to seat, are commonly represented (Figs 3 and 4, see pp. 17, 19), often with a low footstool. Sometimes the chair itself is on a plinth, sometimes very short legs. As for tables (Figs 3, 4 and 7, see pp. 17, 19, 27), the materials used were a variety of woods, with scope for decoration in precious wood or precious metal. Marble table tops were to be found in the better sort of home, and shale was commonly used in Britain. Wicker chairs were certainly used in the later Empire. Almost needless to say, the Romans had simple four-square stools and benches, although the favoured number for table legs was three.

With so many diversions to offer, it is easy to see what a blessing the baths must have been to Roman towns, especially to those for whom the comforts of home were limited. They were places even the poorest could find warmth, comfort, company and entertainment. Not every establishment, of course, ran to exercise grounds, swimming pools and recreation rooms, but it is a fact that where you found Romans, you find bathhouses – from the cities of Asia Minor, civilised and cultured before Rome started throwing her weight around, to the windswept moors of Northumbria. Even the tiny garrison of Mediobogdum, high at the exposed top of Hard Knott Pass, possibly the most vicious in England (the views are marvellous, but it must have been a dreaded posting), had its bathing complex.

Before strolling home to dinner, let us consider very briefly how it was that the Romans were able to build such huge and durable monuments. One vital development was their understanding of the true arch, and therefore the dome – a development the Greeks never made, and which limited the size and scope of their buildings. Another was their use of a version of concrete, and detailed understanding of what was then available to be known of materials science. We know a great deal about Roman theory, as well as observable practice, particularly from the works of Vitruvius, who wrote a detailed textbook-cum-sales pitch for Augustus, *On Architecture*, covering everything from town planning to preparation of stucco, symmetry to civil engineering, building materials to hydraulics. The light source for baths, we note, should be the winter west, and for picture galleries the north (still considered appropriate for artists) (I.2.6). The cement was an aggregate, with sand and lime the vital components. Vitruvius emphasises the necessity for the purity of the ingredients (II.4.1 ff.), and particularly recommends *pozzolana*, a volcanic ash from the Vesuvius region, for its strengthening qualities, and also because it sets under water (II.6.1). Other favoured materials included the volcanic rock tufa, limestone, and marble from Carrara – still used to this day (II.7.1 ff.). It was said of Augustus that he found Rome brick and left her marble (well, actually he said it himself [Suetonius, *Augustus*, 28]), but that was not quite as magnificent as it sounds. Thin sheets of marble were used as facings – and have been removed over the centuries, so that the original brick, tufa and limestone can still by observed in Rome by any visitor. The brickwork itself can indeed be awe-inspiring in its skill and scale, and attractively set. The diamond-patterned *opus reticulatum* became the norm by the late Republic. The earlier style, *opus incertum*, which was more roughly set into the concrete core, was actually commended by Vitruvius as being stronger, though less pleasing to the eye (II.8.1). The insecurity of the *insulae*, that we have already considered, was added to by the frequently inadequate building methods and materials, one of the factors which induced Augustus to limit their height to 70 feet. Whether he had anything to do with causing it or not, after the great fire in Rome, Nero brought in very sensible legislation for stronger building methods (Tacitus, *Annals*, XV.53).

We cannot quite see the afternoon sun go down without noting some of the other places whither a Roman might repair for amusement and relaxation. The horrors of the arena are too well-known to require further elaboration here: the gladiatorial contests, wild beast hunts and variations on such themes. The popular theatre, as we have already suggested, could be scarcely less bloody.

Magnificent theatres, built to accommodate performances of tragedy and comedy (both under Greek influence) adorn many a city of Roman times. Asia Minor affords some particularly spectacular examples of Greek towns with theatres built or modified to Roman design, most instantly characterised by the change from the circular *orchestra* (dancing-floor) of the Greeks (in front of the low stage), to the Roman semi-circle, e.g., at Pergamum, Aspendos or Ephesus. Comfort in these great stone theatres was assured: the audience would bring their own cushions, but awnings would be stretched out to protect them from the sun, and there were even sprinklers for scented water. Posters at the Great Theatre in Pompeii announced the days when these would be operating. Few Romans, however, wrote tragedy, and the performance of the works of living playwrights died out in the time of Claudius. The two great Roman comic playwrights, Plautus and Terence, who wrote following the style, and indeed plots, of Greek New Comedy, belong to the early second century BC.

The popular theatrical forms, mimes and farces that replaced serious drama (mime in Roman terms is not a silent art) had their jolly side, in farces of infidelity and the like, but had also a very dark aspect. Nudity and torture might sound like a recipe for the modern emetic genre of horror films, but the Roman versions owed nothing to special effects. The real modern parallel is not the video-nasty, but the snuff-movie. Not every popular drama descended to such levels, but it is horrifying enough that *any* did. The mime was a peculiarly Roman form, in which an actor mimed the story, with a backing choir singing in the background. Although acting was not strictly speaking respectable, actors could become very fêted.

By way of light relief, the populace could go to the races, both ordinary horse-races and, especially, chariot races. The teams, the Blues and the Reds, the Whites and the Greens, were followed with all the fanaticism of certain modern football fans – and with some of the same results. The Romans had to deal with the chariot-racing hooligan. They also had their public order problems with the gladiatorial games – there was such a serious riot in and around the amphitheatre in Pompeii in AD 59 between the Pompeiians and rival supporters from neighbouring Nuceria (depicted in a wall-painting from the city) that it was closed for ten years on the emperor's orders.

Not only were the races thoroughly exciting to watch, and an occasion for the gambling of which the Romans were passionately fond, they were also good places to get to know a lady, as Ovid makes clear in *Amores*, III.2, in which he recreates all three excitements at once.

When they put their minds and money to it, the Romans could throw a remarkable spectacle – even flooding the Campus Martius for a mock naval battle. Echoes of these entertainments can be found in the extravaganzas of the Renaissance princes. The cultured classes, however, retained their taste for the gentler pleasures of music and the private performance of a book.

Let us assume that the master and mistress of our chosen household, their offspring, their freedmen and other clients, have had a quieter time at their ablutions and related pastimes. Be it to rubble-based jerry-built *insula*, comfortable apartment or maisonette (sizeable homes were sometimes divided up for letting), or solid senatorial villa, the bathers must now fasten on their leather boots and shoes and head for home, or tavern, or host, for the main event of the day – dinner.

Evening

The ninth hour, or perhaps the tenth, was the regular dinner time. Dinner (*cena*) was the focus of Roman social, and indeed, home life, as it will be in many a culture where there is time to eat, to converse, to be entertained, and no other distractions.

Unlike in Athens, where women were excluded unless there was only family present, Roman women took their place alongside their menfolk, and even their children, and could have just as much of a say in the inviting of guests. The refusal to do this amicably was one example of the bickering that punctuated Cicero's brother's rather troubled marriage (*Letters to Atticus*, V.1). Let us suppose that things are going a little more gently in our household: the guests are expected, the kitchen is buzzing with work, the tables are being prepared, wine is being drawn. The hosts are preparing to dress for dinner – this too was Roman custom. They dressed down, in a sense, rather than up. The toga was not worn (except at the emperor's table), but rather a lighter garment, called a *synthesis*, which the guest would either bring along with him (or have his slave bring it for him), or which the host would provide. If the guests were clients rather than peers, the latter course would be more likely. Light sandals would be worn in the house, rather than the heavier street shoes or boots, and the diners would take their places barefoot.

Let us have a look at what would be going on in the kitchen. A sizeable household might employ several cooks, each skilled in different arts, just as a modern restaurant might have chefs skilled in different branches of cuisine: entrées, pastry, etc.. There would also be waiters, and even a trained carver (*scissor*), who might prepare the food into suitable spoon- or finger-sized chunks off-stage, or put on a grand show in front of the guests as Trimalchio's does in the *Satyricon* (36).

Roman food could be extraordinarily elaborate (as well as elegantly simple) as we shall see, but the kitchen where it was prepared was a simple place (Fig. 13). Charcoal or wood fires were lit inside the brick structure of the stove, and could be fed or fanned at will. Cooking could be done on the heated surfaces, or over naked flame, e.g., for grilling, and in an oven, for roasting or baking. Roasting could also be done over an open flame.

Just as the eruption of Vesuvius interrupted plans to eat lunch, so it interrupted the cooks, and kitchens have been found at Pompeii and Herculaneum, left as if the cook had just gone out to the store-room for a moment, with all the equipment laid out for use. The House of the Vettii in Pompeii, for example, boasted a fine collection of bronze cooking vessels, while the House of the Stags at Herculaneum gives us examples of earthenware cookware. Pottery was the commonest material because, although it does break, it is cheap and easy to replace – and it is also better than metal for slow cooking, for example, of stews.

Figure 13.   A Roman kitchen.

Bronze was the most usual material for metal cookware, but iron and pewter utensils have also been found. The vessels could not only be functional, but beautiful as well: strainers with the holes arranged in decorative patterns and saucepans with ornate handles turn up from Pompeii to Britain. Ladles, cleavers and other kitchen knives, occasionally (though rarely) two-pronged forks, spoons, deep saucepans, flat pans, frying-pan-shaped vessels (*paterae*) and chafing dishes on feet are among the regular types of cookware. Pompeii has also produced a square pan with indents (from the House of Panza) which looks like an egg-poacher, and a shovel-shaped flat sheet, which reminds one of the implements used by bakers or pizza-chefs. With jugs, pails, large two-handled amphorae for storage, and even an elegant kettle on a stand, the Roman kitchen had plenty of equipment which, although simple, was more than adequate for the production of fine food.

A well-known piece of cooking apparatus from Pompeii is a fine bronze example of a *thermospodium* (Fig. 13, see p. 68), a kind of elaborate samovar-type device for keeping liquids, perhaps mulled wine, warm. It stands on a tray on elaborate legs (zoomorphic base crowned with winged human figures). At one corner, an urn contained the liquid which then passed through a channel into the hollow walls of a round fire-box beside it, where it would be heated. At the side of the fire-box is a tap for drawing off the liquid. The tray held the spare fuel, and the ashes could be cleaned into it. The whole is not only a practical tool, but also a decorative piece of furniture, and as such must have been for use in the dining-room (*triclinium*) rather than the kitchen – there is not much point in heating your wine if it is going to cool down on its way from the kitchen.

The Roman larder would contain a selection of items familiar and not-so-familiar today. Basics like pulses (beans of various sorts and chick peas) were a staple. Grains included not only wheat, in which Italy had ceased to be self-sufficient by the late Republic, but also spelt (an archaic variety of wheat now rarely grown but still to be found in Germany and France) and barley. These two formed the basis of breads (especially for the poorer classes, but perfectly tasty and nutritious) and soups or gruels. Pastry was used to make pastries, to act as a thickening ingredient (like a roux), or to encase meat for baking, as it were, *en papillote*.

Liquid ingredients included a variety of cooking wines. Ordinary drinking-wines were sometimes used, but for cooking purposes specialised wines were more usual, including *passum*, a musky raisin wine; *mulsum*, a honey and wine mixture; various reductions of must (the juice from crushed grapes, sometimes with fruit or flower flavours) and honey-water (*hydromel*). All these were used in savoury recipes as well as sweet. The Romans had the same taste that is to be found in mediaeval food for combining the sweet and savoury in one dish.

Something no Roman kitchen could be without was the indispensible fish-sauce, *garum*, the basic sauce, or *liquamen*, the strained liquid, made of fermented fish entrails. This condiment appears as commonly in Roman cooking as soy sauce in Chinese or Japanese dishes. Where the Romans went it had to go too, and it was transported around the Empire in huge quantities.

The process of making *liquamen* sounds disgusting, and the ubiquitous fish-sauce was something of a mystery to many a food historian, who failed to see the attraction, until recently. The growth of interest in the food of the Far East has actually reintroduced *liquamen* as something available to most of us at any well-stocked oriental grocer, for in Vietnam (where it is known as *nuoc mam*) and in Thailand (where is is known as *nam pla*) exactly the same sauce, made from the juices of fermented fish, is in use every day. This is a great relief to anyone who wishes to try Roman cookery but would prefer not to share a home with a barrel of rotting mackerel guts. *Liquamen* production was big business for the Romans, and various grades were made, the most expensive from the livers of red mullet, a favourite fish.

Herbs and spices were used in profusion. Some of these could be provided from the garden, others were hugely expensive imports. The Romans had the money, the contacts, and the power to indulge their food whims. Some seasonings are as common today: pepper, ginger, coriander, thyme, oregano and celery seed are just some examples. Others, while still to be found in a good herb garden, are more familiar as ingredients of mediaeval or Elizabethan cookery, or even herbal medicines: lovage, pellitory-of-the-wall, pennyroyal, rue and elecampane. There are others that we are unlikely to come across at all: mastic, spikenard and silphium. Mastic is a kind of resin from the pistachio nut tree, still used in the Middle East; spikenard, a favourite scenting agent for the ancient Egyptians, was imported from the Eastern Mediterranean and India – laurel is a reasonable substitute; silphium or laser was the product of a kind of giant fennel which was so popular it became extinct in North Africa by the first century AD. The Romans themselves used asafoetida as a substitute for silphium, and this is readily available from Indian grocers, as it is a regular ingredient of Indian food, and from herbalists. The huge range of flavourings available to and used by the Romans cannot be covered here, but they well understood the art of blending large numbers of ingredients to create just the right taste, and were prepared to go to the ends of the earth to get what they wanted.

This last point illustrates one of the reasons why the study of food is such a fascinating one. Not only is food inherently interesting, but the sophistication of a society's eating habits, the range of ingredients it uses and whence they are obtained, questions of production and distribution, all these are indicators of that society's wealth, development, contacts, trading power, strength or vulnerability of its agricultural infrastructure and attendant pressures, and so on. Remember that Italy was *not* self-sufficient in food production, and that there was an urban mob to keep pacified, and consider how such factors must have influenced the perceptions of those who ruled Rome.

Many vegetables and fruits that one would expect to find in a modern Italian kitchen and garden would also have been used by the Romans, with certain notable exceptions: the tomato and the pepper and other New World vegetables were not to be known in Italy for many centuries to come.

Fish and shellfish were available in plenty and in great variety from an as yet unpolluted Mediterranean, as imports from as far afield as the oyster beds of England, and from inland lakes and rivers. Meats ranged from the everyday, such as chicken, pork or kid, to game when available – venison, boar, hare or pheasant for example – to what we would consider the frankly outrageous, such as dolphin, flamingo or capon's testicles, and including parts of of the animal many of us would have no desire to reach. Flamingo tongues and peacock's brains belong to the absurdly over-indulgent end of the market, but what the delicate might regard as truly awful offal, formed part of an everyday diet. Stuffed sow's udder, as one example, is however no more revolting than the Scottish haggis, or Hungarian stuffed stomach. Sausages were great favourites, and the much-prized Lucanian sausage, of force-meats with herbs, spices and nuts, was used not only on its own but as an ingredient for other dishes. Snails were eaten on their own or in stuffings, and a characteristic elegant form of spoon, the *cochlear*, with a pointed end to the handle, was used for extracting them from their shells. Snails were farmed, as were dormice (the edible dormouse, *glis glis*). Indeed the skill in farming snails was so great that it was claimed that it was possible to produce monsters whose shells could contain twenty pints (Pliny, *Natural History*, IX.82). Apicius gives a recipe for stuffed dormice, and dormice in honey formed part of the hors d'oeuvres at Trimalchio's blow-out.

Roman food ranged from simple baked egg-custard or sole poached in wine to stomach stuffed with minced pork, brains, eggs, nuts, herbs and spices, baked, smoked and boiled again. Cake recipes range from a meandering set of instructions for a cheese and herb cake from the redoubtable Cato, more normally known as the epitome of Roman virtues like *gravitas* (though not here *brevitas*), in *De Re Rustica* (LXXVI.1-4), which would not only take a page or so of an average cookery book, but from the sounds of things most of the day, to very quick and easy fried pastries in honey from Apicius. (To be fair, Cato does give some less daunting recipes as well as advice on human and veterinary medicine, estate management, guard dogs, tree training, how to mix wall plaster, and many fascinating insights into country life, which must lie beyond the scope of this book.) Unfortunately, there appears to be a missing book on pastries from Apicius' fascinating work, so, although references to sweets and pastries abound, recipes are few and far between.

Before proceeding to the dining-room, let us look at some examples of the sorts of menus the cook and the kitchen-slaves, or in a poorer home the wife and mother, would be working on.

One simple meal in a poor household is described by Ovid in the tale of Philemon and Baucis, who entertained the gods una-wares (*Metamorphoses*, VIII.630 ff.). Baucis scurries to prepare as best a meal as she can – boiled bacon with cabbage, fresh mint, endives and radishes, olives, a kind of 'brandied cherry', cheese and eggs baked in their shells for a first course, followed by nuts, figs, dates, plums, apples, grapes and a honeycomb. It is not bad going for a poor old couple, but this is poetry, and furthermore this is fresh produce which should be available on a decent small-holding. The scene is from country life, and we are concerned with the urban sprawl of Rome itself, but it is a fair example of Roman tastes.

The satiric poets write about food rather a lot, perhaps because they felt their supplies of it were not as secure as they could wish. Martial invites his friend Toranius to share a simple supper – one he is not likely to get fat on (V.78). He offers lettuce, leeks and tunny with sliced eggs for starters, followed by broccoli, bacon, beans and sausage with white pudding, then for dessert, raisins, pears and roasted chestnuts. But just assuming that there might be room for a little more (and Martial reckons this is pretty poor fare), then he can offer olives, lupin seeds and chick peas.

Contrast these simple, but perfectly appetising meals with the reputed greed and extravagance of the Emperor Vitellius, one of those who have given Roman dining a bad name by banqueting four times a day, drinking heavily and getting through the whole overstuffing process by vomiting regularly. He had a habit of landing himself on unfortunate hosts who had then to provide feasts at staggering expense. One of these, given by his brother, achieved particular fame. Amongst its dishes were 2,000 fish and 7,000 game birds, but pride of place went to a specially created recipe, with ingredients collected from across the Empire, which included pike livers, brains of pheasant and peacock, flamingo tongues and lamprey milt (Suetonius, *Vitellius*, 13). This obscene indulgence should be seen as an aberration rather than normality. The master race had money and leisure to indulge food fads and oneupmanship, but even some of their more esoteric tastes are actually not so different from other cuisines of history and indeed of modern continental Europe today.

The most famous feast of them all, however, is that magnificent triumph of new money over taste – the *cena Trimalchionis*, Tri-malchio's banquet, the best known, and funniest, part of Petronius' novel, *The Satyricon*. (Petronius was Nero's *arbiter elegantiae*, master of ceremonies and arbiter of taste, though not, according to Tacitus, a depraved sensualist like his Emperor, but rather a man of charm, in the best sense, who made a study of idle luxury – a Beau Brummel, or one of the more intelligent members of the Drones' Club [*Annals*, XVI.17]).

Sticking for the moment strictly to the menu for the extraordinary meal, we begin with the hors d'oeuvres (*gustatio*): olives, dormice in honey and poppy seeds, sausages with damsons and pomegranate seeds, 'peahens' eggs' – actually made of pastry stuffed with figpeckers (little birds) in egg yolk and pepper (life is still a hazardous business for song birds in Italy, annually slaughtered in vast numbers), all washed down with honey wine. For entrées (*fercula*) Trimalchio was not going to be satisfied with good plain food. A main dish was arranged as the signs of the Zodiac with appropriate foods – Aries: beans; Taurus: beef; Gemini: testicles and kidneys; Cancer: a wreath; Leo: African figs; Virgo: sterile sow's udder; Libra: a set of scales holding a tart in one and a cake in the other; Scorpio: lobster; Sagittarius: a bull's eye; Capricorn: some other kind of crustacean or horned fish; Aquarius: goose; and Pisces: two mullets. Contained within this circle were roasted well-fattened fowl, sows' udders, hare (decorated with wings) and four miniature fountains in the shape of Marsyas (flayed alive by an indignant Apollo for daring to challenge his musical prowess), sending out a stream of peppered *liquamen*. The food was carved at table by Trimalchio's *scissor*, and served with bread and Falernian (the best) wine, which Trimalchio claimed was a hundred years old – it would have been undrinkable. Storage methods were not up to preserving vintages for such a length of time, although mature wines were certainly appreciated.

The essence of refinement may pehaps be to know when enough is enough, and less is more. Trimalchio was not refined. Next on the menu comes a huge wild boar, with baskets of fresh Syrian and dried Theban dates hanging from its tusks, encompassed about with suckling piglets made of cake (take-home presents) and stuffed with live thrushes – just as live birds would be placed in a 'coffin' or pastry case in mediaeval times, which would be put in the oven just long enough to cook the pastry, and then the birds would fly free as the pie was carved, as in the rhyme about four-and-twenty blackbirds. Fortunately there was a lot of conversation and side-shows going on, because this meal is not over yet – we are still on the second course. Live pigs were paraded around, then one chosen to be slaughtered, and stuffed with sausages and blood puddings, which poured out like entrails when the pig was later sliced open in front of the guests. Last but not least of the dishes of the *fercula*, a boiled calf wearing a helmet was carved up by a servant dressed as Ajax (who slaughtered a field of sheep in a fit of madness, mistaking them for the enemy).

There was not much chance to draw breath before dessert (*mensa secunda*), however, as cakes, apples and grapes smothered in saffron were quickly produced, the fruits nestling in the well-endowed lap of a pastry Priapus. The savouries were not modest little bites either – a fat capon apiece, rather than a more normal songbird, and goose eggs in pastry. While all this is going on, Trimalchio describes yet another dinner – a rather more modest affair of a funeral feast particularly enlivened by the presence of bear-meat on the menu. All is not yet over in his own extravaganza, however. There is more – 'thrushes' of pastry stuffed with nuts and raisins, quinces stuck with thorns to look like sea-urchins, a fat goose surrounded by fish and game – apparently, it was all made of pork. Finally there were oysters, scallops, and last of all, snails. The rest of the entertainment was just as grotesque.

This is, of course, satire, but satire has to be based on reality or it is neither biting nor funny, and the example of Vitellius' gross over-indulgence is of a piece with Trimalchio's ghastly banquet. The more usual meal was of fresh herbs and vegetables, meat or fish, eggs, cheese and fruit, served in reasonable proportions, and shared with friends (but it must be said, Vitellius was not the only Roman to vomit part-way through a meal in order to get the rest down).

Let us assume that our household affects the more restrained sort of fare, and that the family and their guests are looking forward to an evening of good food and genteel entertainment – a contrast Pliny makes between the evening he offered and the one his friend Septicius chose (*Letters*, I.15). Instead of a meal of lettuce, snails, eggs, barley cake, with, amongst other delicacies, olives, beetroots, gherkins and onions, washed down with honey wine chilled in snow (in Apicius and elsewhere snow is mentioned as a chilling agent), and accompanied by a comic play, a reader or a singer (which is a reasonable example of a normal evening's entertainment in the better sort of house), he chose to go else-where to sample oysters, sow offal, sea-urchins and Spanish dancing-girls – in the last case the sampling may well have gone beyond just watching them dance.

The *triclinium*, with its arrangement of couches (Fig. 14), would come into its own at dinner-time – the mid-day meal would not be taken reclining. A sizeable house might boast more than one *triclinium*, even including, as we have already seen, an outdoors dining area. The House of Loreius Tiburtinus or the House of the Ephebe at Pompeii provide attractive examples.

As an important public room, the *triclinium* would merit expensive decoration, again in the intense colours noted earlier in the bedroom, particularly in the 'Third Style', with its small motifs and detailed friezes set against washes of black or the deep, brown-toned 'Pompeiian' red, or sometimes yellow, and in the 'Fourth Style' with its busy theatrical scenes and fantastical architecture. The 'Second Style', which is more realistically architectural, gives more sense of space, as the central division of the tripartite arrangement that characterised Roman walls would

Figure 14.   At dinner.

seem to open out into real space, however mythological the scene depicted. The oldest style, the 'First', is the simplest, with mock-marbling effects rather than architectural detail or figurative work.

Even an indoors dining-room would tend to open off the garden in a villa, both to use the light source, and in order to enjoy the sights and scents. As evening fell, however, lights would be required. Roman lamps burned the essential olive oil, the importance of which in Roman life and economy must now be plain. Terracotta lamps have been found in profusion from one end of the Empire to the other, sometimes fairly plain, but often decorated with scenes in low relief. The were shaped rather like covered gravy boats, with a hole in the top for filling, and one or more spouts for the wick(s). Examples have been found with and without handles. Terracotta is the most common medium, mass-produced in moulds, but examples in metal, bronze or gold, have also been found. One or more lamps could be set on high candelabra, delicate columns of three to five feet in height, standing on the favoured number of three low legs, on which a lamp would stand, or from which several could be suspended. The candelabrum which had to carry more weight would be a more substantial, and highly-decorated affair, with fluted columns, zoomorphic feet and detailed carvings on the plinth. Some lamps come with integral low stands. Portable lanterns were also used, with translucent horn where we would now use glass. The humble candle and simple candlestick also had their place.

The scene thus illuminated would be of three wide couches, slightly higher towards the table than at the back, well plumped up with mattresses and bolsters and each able to accommodate three reclining diners, set round three sides of a square, with the fourth side open for the slaves to come in and serve. Either one large square table or individual tables before each place would be set. Plates and bowls, be they in humble pottery or precious silver, would be set for the guests, along with knives, toothpicks (Trimalchio's, of course, was silver), and spoons (forks were only used in the kitchen, if at all, and were not to become normal tableware in Italy until Renaissance times). The Roman spoon is an elegant creation with its elongated bowl, and delicate handle with the pointed tip for winkling out snails. Cups, goblets or beakers for the wine would also be laid out, and the slaves would be busy keeping guests supplied from their jugs. Glass was used as well as pottery and metals for tableware, both for eating and serving.

The guests are arriving now, and must be attended to by the slaves, their feet washed, for sandals were removed before one took one's place on the dinner couch, and if necessary a *synthesis* provided. Trimalchio's slaves even threw in a little pedicure for good measure (*Satyricon*, 31).

The order of seating was very formal. The top couch was the one in the middle, the *lectus medius*, and on it the place of honour, the consular place, was the right-hand end, which was the sixth in the order of progress round the table, which started at the left-hand end of the left couch, the *lectus summus*, and worked its way round to the lowliest position, the ninth, at the right-hand end of the right couch, the *lectus imus*. A guest of the highest importance, such as the Emperor, would occupy the top couch alone, but on the whole that would be rather bad form. A large party would require more sets of couches, and would be based on multiples of nine.

Originally, women had eaten sitting rather than reclining, and there are frescoes and relief dinner scenes showing them thus, either seated at the end of the couch or in a separate chair, but it became normal for women also to recline alongside the male guests. Ovid notes, as he would, the opportunities such proximity might present for a little entertainment extra to that provided by the host (*Amores*, I.4), and indeed as the evening wears on, in certain settings, the couches obviously proved a temptation – a relief carving of a dinner party shows one of the women already overtaken by slumber while the others carry on drinking. Ovid warns of the fate that might befall the young woman overcome by drink (*Ars Amatoria*, III.764-8) – not only is it a very disagreeable sight, he complains, but it is also an open invitation to the men in the group (he preferred to make his invitations to the wide-awake). Ovid and his ilk went to wilder parties than the one being held at our household. The children are also to be present, and they will be seated on stools by the couches. A boy would not recline until he had donned the *toga virilis*.

Much of the food was eaten with the fingers, so it was important to eat delicately – another warning from Ovid in the same part of the *Ars Amatoria* (III.754 f.) is to be dainty in picking up one's food, and avoid smearing it all over one's face. Slaves would also be standing ready to wash the diners' hands, before, during and after the meal. Another sign of Trimalchio's vulgar extravagance was that he had his guests' hands washed with wine.

The great wine-producing area of Roman Italy was Campania, where the rich volcanic soils nourished the favourite vintages. In fact, half the wine drunk in Rome came from the region. The most famous of them all was the Falernian, but the wines of other localities were also appreciated for their qualities – Setine, Caecuban and Alban were others that were particularly prized. Wine was big business too – an estimated half-a-million amphorae a year (at about seven gallons to the amphora, they were so heavy they had to be carried by two men, suspended from poles) were exported to Gaul. The different wines came in slightly different shapes of amphora, with the merchant's name stamped on the handle. They were sealed with cork and wax or resin. The Elder Pliny included a book on viticulture (XIV) in his massive *Natural History*, which continued to be used as a textbook for many centuries.

Roman wines were heavy and sweet, and were never drunk unmixed – not in good company at any rate. At a dinner or drinking party (*commissatio*, which could follow dinner), the *arbiter elegantiae*, master of ceremonies, would decree the proportions in which the wine and water should be mixed, and how many cups were to be drunk.

And so dinner would proceed. We have already seen what some of the entertainment might be – music, a reading, dancing girls, acrobats, good conversation and gossip. Horace has left us a sketch of the banter over the lamplit drinking, as one of the party is teased about his love life (*Odes*, I.27). First the name of the woman is dragged out of him, then he is told how much of a mistake he is making. Some things never change. Horace also describes a piece of unscheduled dinner party entertainment in *Satire*, II.8: Nasidienus, the host, had been boring his guests with details of his gourmet knowledge when suddenly an awning collapsed on top of them, leaving the guests in agonies of stifled laughter.

In their music, as in so much else, the Romans were much indebted to the Greeks, who were the great musical theoreticians. They shared the same kinds of instruments on the whole: lyres

Figure 15. Propping up the bar, the Roman way.

(with often a tortoiseshell as a sounding box), flutes (more like the modern higher-pitched woodwinds than the modern flute), double-pipes, pan-pipes (i.e., with graded lengths of pipe), trumpets and horns, cymbals and tambourines. A mosaic of musicians from Pompeii, for example, shows a female with the double-pipe and two garlanded men with tiny cymbals like temple bells and a large tambourine the size of an Irish drum (bodhran). The water organ was popular in Roman times.

Meanwhile, those without grand dining-rooms and the wherewithal for formal parties would be eating quietly at home, lingering over the varied pleasures of the baths, or heading for the taverns and other places of nocturnal entertainment.

A glass of wine drawn from the pitchers set into the marble counter of the *thermopolium* or bar (Fig. 15), and something hot for dinner, such as the *offellae* we have already seen being totted up on the walls of the Herculaneum Suburban Baths, would go down well. Apicius gives some recipes for *offellae* hot and cold. They might be likened to kebabs, pieces of meat often marinaded in herbs and spices. The very simplest are fried in fish sauce and honey, but others require more elaborate preparation.

After fortifying himself thus a man might be looking for some more energetic diversion. He might have to look no farther than the tavern itself. The Taverna Lusoria at Pompeii had for its inn sign a vessel flanked by a phallus on either side, and while the phallus could carry an innocent tutelary meaning, it clearly did not do so here. In Roman Ephesus the way to the local brothel is marked in the street with an equally unequivocal female sign and a footprint.

The Romans were far from coy about sex. Ovid may allegedly have been banished for writing immoral poetry (a more political motive is suspected), but his erotic poetry, although certainly X-certificate stuff, was hardly worse than his contemporaries, who also wrote on love, lust and loss, or the earlier Catullus, whose mixture of touching beauty and vicious foul-mouthed vulgarity has occasioned anxious moments to many a delicately-minded scholar. Even Horace contains passages once considered unsuitable for translation. Erotic poetry was an accepted literary genre, and good clean fun it seems as compared with Roman ideas of public entertainment.

Erotic imagery of a pictorial kind was everywhere – in reliefs, in paintings, in mosaics, in statues, in decorative tableware, or lamps, even on sarcophagi. A house of ill-repute, such as the Lupanare beside Sittius' inn at Pompeii, had its dirty pictures, but, executed with appropriately varying levels of artistry, erotic scenes were to be found as an everyday feature of entirely respectable homes, just as entirely respectable homes today might contain a nude in painting or statuary and think nothing of it. Admittedly, the Roman versions tended to involve a measure of activity, detail, and combinations, male–female, male–male, human–animal, that we are not entirely used to.

The accommodation for amorous entertainment could be rather basic – little cubicles with only a curtain to provide a modicum of privacy, or more discreet rooms upstairs. The prostitute touting for custom in the streets could be recognised by her toga. Prostitutes had to be registered – they even had a craft guild – and had to pay taxes in the amount of the fee from a single encounter. Gaius (Caligula) brought this particular measure in to help refill his emptying coffers, and he even insisted that those who had given up the game and got married had to pay – but then he was not a man known for consideration and restraint (Suetonius, *Gaius*, 40). He even opened his own brothel at one point, forcing married women and free-born boys to work there – the scandal lies in their status, not sex (*Gaius*, 41). But these are the reputed excesses of one mad emperor. Daily (and nightly) business went on in Rome – and everywhere else – without causing public outcry. Petronius affords us a glimpse into this world in the *Satyricon*, in which Encolpius, while madly in love with his slave-boy Giton, also has encounters with ageing prostitutes, apparently delightful young girls, rapacious women, and the odd witch. The Romans did not draw a clear dividing line between homosexuality and hetero-sexuality – the dividing line was between active and passive partner – and a love poem could as well be written to a ravishing boy as to a ravishing girl.

Catullus' Lesbia may have been a high-born lady, Clodia, but it is likely that Propertius' Cynthia, Tibullus' Delia and Horace's Lydia, with their Greek names (not, of course, necessarily their own) may well have been courtesans, higher up the scale than the street girls or tavern girls, rather than ladies of quality hiding behind pseudonyms.

Apart from these outlets, a Roman householder might find his extra-curricular entertainment for free in his household slaves. Horace certainly recommends this as a safe and comfortable alternative to adultery, in *Satire*, I.2. Formal concubinage was also a possibility, but this would not be expected to be combined with marriage to someone else. The idea of chastity for a man did not enter into the scheme of things, but formal arrangements were another matter.

That all this activity did not result in a population explosion is plain from the fact that Augustus felt constrained to produce a series of laws aimed at promoting family life among the citizens – disabilities on the unmarried and privileges for those with three or more children. Apart from some noble, old-fashioned and lucky couples like Drusus and Antonia (parents of Germanicus and Claudius, amongst others) who had a large family, and in this case it was the husband who died young, there was a shortage of freeborn children in Rome. Problems of infertility and mis-carriage, lead-poisoning, perinatal death (of mother and children) – one of Pliny's saddest letters records the deaths of two sisters in childbirth (IV.21) – these were natural hazards. There were other unnatural hazards for a child. Abortion was common. We have already seen Juvenal noting the advantage of a eunuch lover in this respect. Ovid, on the other hand, lashes out angrily at women who abort their children (*Amores*, II.14) just to keep their sto-machs flat. This was no more a safe process than childbirth, as the poem goes on to note, and could as easily end in death. The father had rights of life and death over his child once born, and could insist that the child be exposed. The extent of infanticide and exposure in Rome is not known. The staple comic plot of an exposed child being reunited with parents and finding true love arises out of Greek rather than Roman custom.

For our knowledge of Roman contraception we are particularly indebted to Soranus, who was trained in Ephesus and worked in Rome in the late first and early second centuries AD. Of his surviving works, his *Gynaecology* was especially important. (There were also women doctors, who attended to women's disorders, as well as midwives.) Methods of contraception, rather than inducing abortion, varied from Pliny the Elder's suggestion of an amulet made up of worms extracted from the body of a hairy spider and wrapped in deer skin (*Natural History*, XIX.27) to the rhythm method (unfortunately Soranus selects precisely the wrong times for abstinence and indulgence), taking in *en route* an assortment of plugs such as wool, and pessaries, and useful advice to the woman such as to hold her breath at the crucial moment. Among the substances a woman might besmear herself with are olive oil, honey, resin, balsam, white lead and alum (*Gynaecology*, I.61). Some of these might indeed have had a measure of effect, but the whole business was none too secure or, one suspects, entirely comfortable.

Whatever carousing may have been going on in the city's hostelries, and before the serious drinking and racier conversation got started at home, our young boy and girl will have been taken off to bed. They must, after all, be up early in the morning to go to school.

Rolling home from the tavern, or from dinner with one's patron, having quaffed as much of his second-best wine as he was willing to allow, and with the Roman equivalent of a doggy-bag (a napkin full of goodies), the drunk, lover or poet might pause to decorate the walls with a few graffiti. Herculaneum, which was a nice town, was not well-supplied with these, but in Pompeii they are everywhere – declarations of love, declarations of hate, maudlin expressions of goodwill and complaints about the wine, all vying for place with the for sale signs and the election posters.

The streets would be far from quiet now, because the sun has set and according to Julius Caesar's law wheeled traffic was allowed. So even if the shopkeepers and daily crowds had gone, there would be the clatter of wooden wheels over paved streets, horses', donkeys' and mules' hooves. Light two-wheeled carriages, ox-carts from the countryside, the larger carriages used for travelling, for example, when the family went south to Campania on holiday, baggage carts with solid wheels – the racket on the main roads must have been frightful. Juvenal complains about being kept awake all night by the rumbling traffic and the risk of broken bones in traffic accidents (III.235 ff.).

The fact that there were people about did not, however, make the streets safe. On the contrary, some of the people who were about were there with the precise intention of making sure they were anything but for the unprotected. Until Augustus set up his fire-brigade, the *vigiles*, there was nothing that could be described as a police force in Rome, and the night was the time of the mugger and the murderer. There was a body called the *triumviri nocturni*, but little is known about them. They certainly did not make their name for posterity by keeping the crime rate down. The *vigiles* combined their very necessary firewatch work with certain policing duties.

There were no street lights to deter unwanted attention, or to light the way. Encolpius, trying to make his way home after Trimalchio's banquet, and decidedly the worse for wear, stumbles off over the stones and broken crockery in the street, having a thoroughly miserable time, lost but for the ingenuity of Giton, who had marked up the way with chalk (*Satyricon*, 79). He made it back to his bed in safety. Right at the beginning of his adventures he had been fearful, as night fell, of pickpockets in a very dubious market-place, where most items were probably stolen (*Satyricon*, 12). As he was himself in possession of stolen goods, that might have served him right. Pickpockets were amongst the less dangerous hazards.

Juvenal fears not only a shower of unpleasant substances, but even death from the debris being thrown out from on high in the *insulae*, including pots. You might fall foul of a drunken bully-boy, spoiling for a fight, or some thieving. Even the existence of the *vigiles* might not prevent you from being beaten up, or even murdered, as there were not enough of them to go around. All in all, rants Juvenal, unless you are rich enough to be carried safely home by your slaves, surrounded by torchlight, then you might as well make your will before venturing out into the streets at night (III.235-310).

The day has been a long one. The guests haul themselves out of the comfort of their couches, call for their shoes and their togas or cloaks, and prepare to brave the streets to go home. Around the house lamps are being extinguished, and in the darkness the scents of the garden steal in. In the *insula* the noise of your neighbours snoring, quarrelling or being sick on the stairs may be heard. The lady retires to her room, where she may be joined for a time by her husband, before he repairs to his room. Before she sleeps, however, she must put on her bread and water face-pack, so that she can face tomorrow the more radiantly. Perhaps, however, the master has work to do, and will sit up in the night reading, learning, preparing. But all eyes must close, even those of the doorkeeper and his dog, at least one with still half an ear cocked for the sound of burglars defying the locks and bolts.

Ostlers ready their charges to set out with the carriages, or settle them after their night's work. In the *insulae* the tenants check their braziers for any last stray and lethal spark. The tradesman living above his shop may take one last look around to check the premises are secure. In their billets and stations the cohorts of *vigiles* check on their duties.

The slaves finish clearing away the remains of the party, yawning as they go. Their couches too await. The 'cats' eyes' in the floor – fluorescent stone as part of the mosaic – might save some stumbles (these can be seen e.g. in the House of the Ceii in Pompeii, where they are still useful to the custodians). And so our household sleeps, sinking into the mattresses, under patterned coverlets, dreaming of the arena, of political power, of romance, or the army, of freedom. The puppy makes the rounds of the accessible beds, leaps onto the end of his master's and curls up contentedly at his feet. Even in Rome, the biggest and the richest city in the known world, a mean city, an overcrowded city, a noisy city, a splendid city, there is, for a time and in this place, peace.

Suggestions for Further Study/Projects

1. Visit Roman sites – the value of actually walking in the streets, touching the buildings, being in the places the Romans lived, cannot, for me, be overestimated. Britain is not well supplied with extant town sites (Roman towns in Britain tend to be still occupied), but there are villa sites, military encampments, and parts of military towns still accessible. Continental Europe, Asia Minor, the Levant and North Africa all contain more in the way of complete town sites. A field trip is highly recommended.

2. Study museum collections and displays – the British Museum, Colchester, Caerleon and the Hadrian's Wall museums are just some that would amply repay a study visit.

3. Read the sources! This is so basic it should hardly need saying, but for the investigation of everyday living some of the sources that are of lesser literary value come into their own. There is no better way to try to comprehend another culture than by reading what it says about itself.

4. Stage a Roman banquet. This is very suitable for group work, when possible, as it falls into various parts covering a range of the subjects raised in this book, and can combine well with more formal studies.

    i. Research and cook a Roman meal.

    ii. Research Roman furniture (reproduction lamps, at least, are not hard to find).

    iii. Research Roman interior decoration.

    iv. Research and make Roman clothes (books on theatrical costume may be of more immediate use than textbooks).

    v. Research Roman jewellery (reproductions can be found).

    vi. Research Roman make-up (but be wary of trying it!).

    vii. Research Roman tableware (there are commercial reproductions available).

    viii. Research Roman musical instruments (there are cassette tapes of 'Roman' music available, but we have a limited knowledge of how it actually sounded).

ix. Provide an entertainment, e.g., part of a play or a recitation (perhaps in conjunction with a Latin-speaking contest).

Suggestions for Further Reading

Translations and Bilingual Texts

Evidence on daily life may be gained from a vast range of sources – clues can be found almost anywhere, but certain kinds of work are particularly useful, because it is in their nature that they deal with everyday things: love poetry, satire, novels, personal letters and practical textbooks on a variety of subjects. The following are particularly helpful and reasonably accessible – this should not be regarded as a complete list, nor as a definitive guide for textual study. This subject is an adjunct to formal studies, and my guiding principle is ease of obtaining information. Many of the translations are well annotated.

Apicius, *The Roman Cookery Book*, trans. Barbara Flower and Elisabeth Rosenbaum, London, 1958. Bilingual.

The Roman Cookery of Apicius, Translated and Adapted for the Modern Kitchen, John Edwards, London, 1984. Contains both straight translation and also tested recipes in modern terms for almost all the dishes (Apicius was writing for professionals, and did not include details of quantity, timing etc. necessary for the amateur to reproduce something edible).

Cato, *On Agriculture*, trans. William Davis Hooper, Loeb Classical Library, London and Cambridge, Mass., 1936. This book has not dealt with country life, but Cato is included for his recipes and other homely detail.

Catullus, trans. Francis Warre Cornish, rev. G. P. Goold, Loeb Classical Library, London and Cambridge, Mass., 1988.

The Poems of Catullus, trans. Peter Whigham, Harmondsworth, 1966.

Cicero, *Letters to Atticus* (three vols), trans. E. O. Winstedt, Loeb Classical Library, London and Cambridge, Mass., 1912-1918. Cicero was a copious correspondent, but these have a particular intimacy and immediacy.

Horace, *Odes and Epodes*, trans. C. E. Bennett, Loeb Classical Library, London and Cambridge, Mass., 1978. These are of more value for their beauty than their information about everyday life, but there are gems of evidence.

Horace, *The Complete Odes and Epodes*, trans. W. G. Shepherd, Harmondsworth, 1983.

Horace, *Satires, Epistles and Ars Poetica*, trans. H. Rushton Fairclough, Loeb Classical Library, London and Cambridge, Mass., 1978.

Horace, *Satires and Epistles* (in the same volume, Persius, *Satires*), trans. Niall Rudd, Harmondsworth, 1973.

Juvenal and Persius, trans. G. G. Ramsay, Loeb Classical Library, London and Cambridge, Mass., 1918.

Juvenal, *The Sixteen Satires*, trans. Peter Green, Harmondsworth, 1967.

Martial, *Epigrams* (two vols), Walter C. A. Ker, Loeb Classical Library, London and Cambridge, Mass., 1968.

Martial, *The Epigrams*, selected and trans. James Michie, Harmondsworth, 1978. Bilingual, but not complete.

Martial, *Epigrams of Martial Englished by Divers Hands*, J. P. Sullivan and Peter Whigham (eds), Berkeley/Los Angeles, 1987. Bilingual. This is probably not so easily come by, but is fun because it includes translations of the complete *Epigrams* from a variety of poets and periods.

Ovid, *The Art of Love and Other Poems*, trans. J. H. Mozley, Loeb Classical Library, London and Cambridge Mass., 1979. Includes *Ars Amatoria, Remedia Amoris, Medicamina Faciei*.

Ovid, *Heroides and Amores*, trans. Grant Showerman, Loeb Classical Library, London and Cambridge, Mass., 1986. Ovid's attempts at high art come over rather as doggerel, so go straight to the *Amores* for some interesting sidelights on everyday life.

Ovid, *The Erotic Poems*, trans. Peter Green, Harmondsworth, 1982.

Petronius, *Satyricon* (includes Seneca, *Apocolocyntosis*, a satire about the Emperor Claudius), trans. W. H. D. Rouse, Loeb Classical Library, London and Cambridge, Mass., 1987.

Petronius, *The Satyricon and the Fragments*, trans. J. P. Sullivan, Harmondsworth, 1969.

Pliny (the Younger), *Letters* (two vols), trans. William Melmoth, rev. W. M. L. Hutchinson, Loeb Classical Library, London and Cambridge, Mass., 1915.

Pliny (the Younger), *Letters and Panegyricus* (two vols), trans. Betty Radice, Loeb Classical Library, London and Cambridge, Mass., 1969.

Pliny, *The Letters of the Younger Pliny*, trans. Betty Radice, Harmondsworth, 1969.

Pliny (the Elder), *Natural History* (ten vols), trans. H. Rackham, W. H. S. Jones, D. E. Eichholz, Loeb Classical Library, London and Cambridge, Mass., 1938 – 1962.

Soranus, *Gynecology*, trans. O. Temkin, Baltimore, 1956.

Suetonius (two vols), trans. J. C. Rolfe, Loeb Classical Library, London and Cambridge, Mass., 1970, 1979.

Suetonius, *The Twelve Caesars*, trans. Robert Graves, rev. Michael Grant, Harmondsworth, 1957, 1979.

Tacitus, *The Annals* (vols III–V of the Loeb *Tacitus*), trans. John Jackson, London and Cambridge, Mass., 1979, 1970, 1969.

Tacitus, *The Annals of Imperial Rome*, trans. Michael Grant, Harmondsworth, 1971.

Virgil, *Eclogues, Georgics, Aeneid* I-VI, trans. J. Rushton Fairclough, Loeb Classical Library, London and Cambridge, Mass., 1978.

Virgil, *The Georgics*, trans. L. P. Wilkinson, Harmondsworth, 1982.

Vitruvius, *On Architecture* (two vols), trans. F. Grainger, Loeb Classical Library, London and Cambridge, Mass., 1970.

Vitruvius, *The Ten Books on Architecture*, trans. Morris Hicky Morgan, New York, 1960.

Rome: The Augustan Age, Kitty Chisholm and John Ferguson, Oxford, 1981. Compiled as an Open University source book, this wide-ranging anthology of translations will be of value to any student of Classical Civilisation.

Greek and Roman Slavery, Thomas Wiedemann, London, 1981. An interesting anthology of texts in translation.

The Roman Household: A Sourcebook, Jane F. Gardner and Thomas Wiedemann, London and New York, 1991. A fascinating anthology.

Background Reading

As this book is necessarily a short one, so is the book list. I include here a selection of works that are enlightening and enjoyable. The reader who wishes to delve more deeply into a specific area will find each of these a useful starting point.

Allason-Jones, Lindsay, *Women in Roman Britain*, London, 1987. Much evidence necessarily derived from the wider Roman world. A very comprehensive, readable work.

Aries, Philippe, and Duby, Georges (eds), *A History of Private Life I. From Pagan Rome to Byzantium*, trans. Arthur Coldhammer, Cambridge, Mass., and London, 1987. A fascinating Gallic approach.

Auguet, Roland, *Cruelty and Civilisation: The Roman Games*, London and New York, 1972 and 1994. An excellent guide to the sort of things the Romans liked doing in their spare time.

de la Bédoyère, Guy, *The Finds of Roman Britain*, London, 1989. A treasure house of reference material.

Balsdon, J. P. V. D., *Life and Leisure in Ancient Rome*, London, 1969. Well-written, and well worth reading.

Balsdon, J. P. V. D., *Roman Women*, London, 1962. Humane and informative.

Bonner, S. F., *Education in Ancient Rome*, London, 1977. Helpful survey.

Brion, Marcel, *Pompeii and Herculaneum. Their Glory and the Grief*, trans. John Rosenberg, London and Salem, 1960. Brion is both professional historian and novelist – a combination of skills that bring these cities vividly to life in this work.

Corson, Richard, *Fashions in Makeup from Ancient to Modern Times*, London, 1972. A huge and comprehensive study.

Carcopino, Jérôme, *Daily Life in Ancient Rome*, Harmondsworth, 1941. A classic, though somewhat humourless.

Deiss, Joseph Jay, *Herculaneum*, New York, 1985. As good a book about Herculaneum as you will find: journalistic, but solidly informative and well-illustrated.

Dill, Samuel, *Roman Society from Nero to Marcus Aurelius*, New

York, 1905. A venerable classic, still worth consulting.

Dixon, Suzanne, *The Roman Mother*, London and Sydney, 1988. Contains much illuminating material.

Embleton, Ronald, and Graham, Frank, *Hadrian's Wall in the Days of the Romans*, Newcastle, 1984. Not always reliable, but the many illustrations are very good.

Finley, M. I., *The Ancient Economy*, London, 1973. Very good introduction to this area of study.

Guhl, E., and Koner, W., *The Greeks and Romans. Their Life and Customs*, London, 1989. Reprint of a typically-detailed nineteenth century work. The mode of expression may be out of date, but the information is sound and extensive.

Greene, Kevin, *The Archaeology of the Roman Economy*, London, 1986. Of interest not only to the archaeologist, but to the economist and historian as well.

Higgins, Reynold, *Greek and Roman Jewellery*, London, 1980. A standard work.

Jackson, Ralph, *Doctors and Diseases in the Roman Empire*, London, 1988. Good introduction to the study of ancient medicine.

Johns, Catherine, *Sex or Symbol. Erotic Images of Greece and Rome*, London, 1982. A serious and scholarly study of attitudes in another culture, and our own distorting perceptions.

Kennedy, E. C., and White, G. W., *S.P.Q.R. The History and Social Life of Ancient Rome*, London, 1965. Although written with the schoolboy of a different generation in mind, it still has value.

Kiefer, Otto, *Sexual Life in Ancient Rome*, New York, 1993. Covers a range of aspects of life in general, and a comprehensive literary survey.

Kraus, T., and von Matt, L., *Pompeii and Herculaneum: The Living Cities of the Dead*, New York, 1975. Excellent work on these cities.

Liversidge, Joan, *Furniture in Roman Britain*, London, 1955. Short, but very useful work for both specialist and general reader.

Meiggs, R., *Roman Ostia*, Oxford, 1960. Very good, especially on housing.

Mossé, Claude, *The Ancient World at Work*, trans. Janet Lloyd, London, 1969. Not as good as Finley, but of use as an introduction.

Olivova, Vera, *Sports and Games in the Ancient World*, trans. D. Orpington, London, 1984. Looks at the place of sports and games in society, as well as the actual activities.

Richter, Gisela, *The Furniture of the Greeks, Etruscans and Romans*, London, 1966. A valuable study.

Robertson, D. S., *Greek and Roman Architecture*, Cambridge, 1943. A standard work.

Singer, Charles, Holmyard, E. J., and Hall, A. R., *A History of Technology*, Oxford, 1954 and 1955. Illuminating.

Soyer, Alexis, *The Pantropheon or A History of Food and Its Preparation in Ancient Times*, New York and London, 1979. Reprint of an exhaustive study by the great chef.

Strong, Donald E., and Brown, David (eds), *Roman Crafts*, London, 1976. Deals with techniques and materials. Very good.

Symons, David J., *The Costume of Ancient Rome*, London, 1987. Brief but comprehensive.

Tanzer, H. H., *The Common People of Pompeii*, Baltimore, 1939. One of the best books on Pompeii.

Toussaint-Samat, Maguelonne, *History of Food*, trans. Anthea Bell, Cambridge, Mass. and Oxford, 1994. Huge, exhaustive, quite fascinating.

Toynbee, J. M. C., *The Art of the Romans*, London and New York, 1965. A good introduction (does not deal with architecture).

Ward Perkins, John and Claridge, Amanda, *Pompeii A.D. 79*, Bristol, 1976. May not be easy to get hold of now, but worth it. Published to accompany the Royal Academy Exhibition in 1976-77, it has an excellent text and invaluable catalogue.

Warde-Fowler, W., *Social Life at Rome in the Age of Cicero*, London, 1916. A companion volume to Dill, and worth consulting for the earlier period, which tends not to receive so much attention.

Wheeler, Mortimer, *Roman Art and Architecture*, London, 1964. Lots of illlustrations, but the text has to be too general for detailed study.

Whitehouse, David, *Glass of the Roman Empire*, New York, 1988. Based on the collection of the Corning Museum of Glass. Very informative.

Wiseman, T. P., *Catullus and His World. A Reappraisal*, Cambridge, 1985. Not just a study of Catullus, but also an excellent study of social life.

Wilson, L. M., *The Clothing of the Ancient Romans*, London, 1938. Helpful reference work.

The Batsford *Everyday Life in...* series is always good value. Several in the series cover aspects of Roman life. The invaluable *Oxford Classical Dictionary* is often a useful first port of call. There is an abundance of picture books, of varying degress of accuracy and attractiveness. One which I am happy to recommend to child or adult is *Ancient Rome*, by Simon James (London, 1990), a British Museum publication with almost no text, but a superb collection of detailed drawings. The well-researched historical novel, while never to be regarded as source material, contrary to the fond belief of some students, can be a good doorway into another culture. The politicking and skullduggery in high places in ancient Rome, as recounted in the scurrilous, gossipy and highly biassed (i.e., highly readable) histories of Suetonius and Tacitus, have been the inspiration for novelists of the calibre of Robert Graves and Allan Massie; even Marius and Sulla have found their way into a novel. The life of the ordinary Roman in the street, however, has not attracted such attention until recently. The Falco novels of Lindsey Davis combine considerable accuracy of detail and excellent yarns.